Concept-Based Language Instruction and Genre-Based Second Language Writing Pedagogy

SECOND LANGUAGE ACQUISITION

Series Editors: **Professor David Singleton**, *University of Pannonia, Hungary* and Fellow Emeritus, *Trinity College, Dublin, Ireland* and **Professor Simone E. Pfenninger**, *University of Zurich, Switzerland*

This series brings together titles dealing with a variety of aspects of language acquisition and processing in situations where a language or languages other than the native language is involved. Second language is thus interpreted in its broadest possible sense. The volumes included in the series all offer in their different ways, on the one hand, exposition and discussion of empirical findings and, on the other, some degree of theoretical reflection. In this latter connection, no particular theoretical stance is privileged in the series; nor is any relevant perspective – sociolinguistic, psycholinguistic, neurolinguistic, etc. – deemed out of place. The intended readership of the series includes final-year undergraduates working on second language acquisition projects, postgraduate students involved in second language acquisition research, and researchers, teachers and policymakers in general whose interests include a second language acquisition component.

All books in this series are externally peer-reviewed.

Full details of all the books in this series and of all our other publications can be found on http://www.multilingual-matters.com, or by writing to Multilingual Matters, BLOCK, The Fairfax, Pithay Ct, Bristol, BS1 3BN, UK.

SECOND LANGUAGE ACQUISITION: 171

Concept-Based Language Instruction and Genre-Based Second Language Writing Pedagogy

Provoking and Assessing Development

J. Elliott Casal, Lindsey M. Kurtz and Xixin Qiu

MULTILINGUAL MATTERS
Bristol • Jackson

DOI https://doi.org/10.21832/CASAL2484

Library of Congress Cataloging in Publication Data
A catalog record for this book is available from the Library of Congress.

Names: Casal, J. Elliott author | Kurtz, Lindsey M. author | Qiu, Xixin author
Title: Concept-Based Language Instruction and Genre-Based Second Language
   Writing Pedagogy: Provoking and Assessing Development / J. Elliott Casal,
Lindsey M. Kurtz and Xixin Qiu.
Description: Bristol; Jackson: Multilingual Matters, 2026. | Series:
   Second Language Acquisition: 171 | Includes bibliographical references
   and index. | Summary: "This book presents an interdisciplinary, flexible
   and comprehensive framework for teaching second language (L2) and
   multilingual writing that integrates Concept-Based Language Instruction
   and Genre-Based Writing Pedagogy. The authors show how L2 writing
   instructors can empower student writers to be agentive, aware and
   strategic in their writing"-- Provided by publisher.
Identifiers: LCCN 2025026997 (print) | LCCN 2025026998 (ebook) |
   ISBN 9781800412439 paperback | ISBN 9781800412484 hardback |
   ISBN 9781800412583 pdf | ISBN 9781800412538 epub
Subjects: LCSH: Language and languages--Study and teaching | Composition
(Language arts)--Study and teaching | Rhetoric--Study and teaching | Multilingualism
Classification: LCC P53.27 .C36 2026 (print) | LCC P53.27 (ebook)
LC record available at https://lccn.loc.gov/2025026997
LC ebook record available at https://lccn.loc.gov/2025026998

British Library Cataloguing in Publication Data
A catalogue entry for this book is available from the British Library.

ISBN-13: 978-1-80041-248-4 (hbk)
ISBN-13: 978-1-80041-243-9 (pbk)

Multilingual Matters
UK: BLOCK, The Fairfax, Pithay Ct, Bristol, BS1 3BN, UK.
USA: Ingram, Jackson, TN, USA.
Authorised Representative: Easy Access System Europe - Mustamäe tee 50, 10621
Tallinn, Estonia, gpsr.requests@easproject.com.

Website: https://www.multilingual-matters.com
X: Multi_Ling_Mat
Bluesky: @multi-ling-mat.bsky.social
Facebook: https://www.facebook.com/multilingualmatters
Blog: https://www.channelviewpublications.wordpress.com

Copyright © 2026 J. Elliott Casal, Lindsey M. Kurtz and Xixin Qiu.

All rights reserved. No part of this work may be reproduced in any form or by any means without permission in writing from the publisher.

The policy of Multilingual Matters/Channel View Publications is to use papers that are natural, renewable and recyclable products, made from wood grown in sustainable forests. In the manufacturing process of our books, and to further support our policy, preference is given to printers that have FSC and PEFC Chain of Custody certification. The FSC and/or PEFC logos will appear on those books where full certification has been granted to the printer concerned.

Typeset by Deanta Global Publishing Services, Chennai, India

Contents

	Acknowledgments	vii
	Foreword	ix
1	Introduction	1
	What This Book Is About	1
	How (and Why) This Book Came to Be	2
	Overview of the Book	3
2	Key Principles and Concepts	7
	Genre-Based Writing Pedagogy	7
	Concept-Based Language Instruction	12
	A Concept-Based Genre Writing Pedagogy Framework	20
3	Legal Writing: Context and Pedagogy	22
	Legal Systems as Languacultures	22
	Legal Analogical Reasoning: A Definition	25
	US Legal Education: A Languaculture	26
	Study Context	29
	The Curriculum	30
	The Concept-Based Genre Writing Curriculum	31
4	Legal Writing: Findings and Implications	38
	Legal Analogical Reasoning	38
	Jun	40
	Discussion and Conclusions	52
5	Graduate Academic Writing: Context, Concepts and Pedagogy	55
	Pedagogical Context and Participants	56
	The Target Concepts	56
	Description of Pedagogy and Data Sources	61
	Analytical Procedures	66
6	Graduate Academic Writing: Findings and Implications	68
	Mona: Agency and Autonomy through Resistance and Creativity	69

	Lucía: Scrutiny, Playfulness and Innovation	77
	Conclusions	81
7	Engineering Writing: Context and Pedagogy	82
	The Target Concepts	83
	Pedagogical Materials Development	87
	Description of Pedagogy and Data Sources	91
	Data Source	94
	Analytical Procedures	96
8	Engineering Writing: Findings and Implications	100
	Geyao's Development of Grammatical Stance Expressions	101
	Geyao's Verbalization in Self-Assessment Activities	107
	Geyao's Verbalization in Stimulated Recalls for Post-Intervention Revisions	110
	Geyao's Definition at the Delayed Interview	114
	Conclusion	115
9	Implications and Considerations for Other Contexts	117
	Emerging Points of Intersection	118
	Practical Questions for Practice	124
	Final Thoughts	132
	References	133
	Index	143

Acknowledgments

Collectively, we are extremely grateful to Multilingual Matters for supporting us in the publication of this book. We also offer our thanks to the faculty we shared at Penn State University for their guidance, expertise, patience, and mediation as we developed these projects. In particular, we must thank Jim Lantolf, for his disarming questions, gracious and generous interest, and contagious wonder and curiosity.

I owe the graduate student participants of my study deep gratitude; we learned so much together during trying times. And thank you to Pejman for the careful review. Thanks to Joseph Lee, Dawn Bikowski, Karen Johnson, and Xiaofei Lu who created spaces for me to think, teach, and learn. Deryn Verity, you saw some value in my crazy ideas and helped me take them seriously. Rebecca Adams and Will Duffy, you are truly empowering colleagues. To my coauthors, thanks for your brilliance, fellowship, patience, and belief that we would pull this off. Nikki, Jackie, Leigh, and Alba, I am honored by and empowered through your love.
– Elliott

A very sincere 谢谢, شكرا لك, and ขอบคุณ to the student participants of my study, who so gamely took every aspect of the curriculum in stride and from whom I learned so very much. Thank you to Tiffany Bennett, who grew to love SCOBAs, and Becky Zoshak, the micro to my macro and still my favorite person to discuss cases with. It's been my good fortune to learn from fantastic teachers and writers. Special thank you to Dorie Evensen, Matt Poehner, and Deryn Verity for your guidance. I also individually thank Jim Lantolf; your voice will forever mediate my thoughts when I write, when I work with students, and when I think about Penn State football. Elliott and Xixin, what a journey it's been and I'm so glad to have learned and developed with the two of you on it. Thank you both for everything. Mom, Dad, Mark – none of what I do is possible without your love, guidance, and support. Thank you.
– Lindsey

I am indebted to my student participants who took a leap of faith, trusting me with engineering writing expertise even when I was not fully convinced of it myself. Fresh from graduation, I am forever grateful to my dissertation committee, Catherine Berdanier, Kevin McManus, Meredith Doran, and Xiaofei Lu. You transformed this project in ways I could not have imagined. And Susan Conrad, thank you for patiently weathering my storms of confusion during the design phase and showing me the priceless possibility that applied linguistics and engineering education could thrive together. To Elliott and Lindsey, who knew a conference presentation could turn into this adventure? Thank you for making my first book-writing journey feel like climbing Mt Nittany with laughter at every turn. And to my parents and Ruge, yes, that mysterious book project I kept raving about for the past year finally materialized!

– Xixin

Foreword

It is a distinct pleasure to have been invited to write a foreword for this unique and important volume. The volume is unique because, to my knowledge, it is the first project that undertakes the integration of three separately conducted doctoral dissertations into a unified pedagogical statement regarding pedagogical practice of any kind. It is also unique because the three dissertations were carried out with very different learner populations: international law students from divergent legal backgrounds learning how to read, interpret, and write legal briefs based on American case law; international graduate students from various L1 backgrounds (Arabic, Chinese, Russian, Korean, Spanish, and Portuguese) learning how to produce research reports in English across an array of academic disciplines ranging from architecture, electrical engineering, and physics, economics and linguistics, all of which have quite different expectations for what constitutes rhetorically acceptable writing; Chinese L1 graduate students enrolled in mechanical engineering programs at two different Chinese universities. To be sure, the authors had to narrow the scope of their respective projects for purposes of the present volume, opting to focus on specific students from their broader research. However, each author describes the specific ways in which they felt it necessary to implement the general pedagogical approach they had adopted for their particular student population and subject matter. This work is important because it demonstrates that the same general pedagogical theory informed by the core principles of the general theory of human psychology proposed by the Russian psychologist L.S. Vygotsky can produce positive developmental outcomes under different contextual circumstances. An especially interesting aspect of the Chinese study is that an earlier attempt by the author to teach academic writing to a group of multilingual Chinese students using a corpus-based tutorial approach was not successful, as the students reported having difficulties 'absorbing' abstract concepts. The follow-up study, using C-BLI, as discussed in Chapters 7 and 8, proved to be much more successful as the students were able to gain control over abstract concepts such as writer stance when producing their own texts.

Vygotsky proposed four core theoretical principles for what is referred to variously as cultural-historical psychology or as sociocultural theory of mind. The principles are designed to explain and understand how the human psyche develops from the dialectical intra-action between biologically evolved mental functions, including, memory, perception, attention, emotion, and survival instinct and the symbolic artifacts, most especially language (but also including numbers, drawings, diagrams, music, etc.), developed by cultural activity over the course of human history. The four principles are sociogenesis, internalization, mediation, and developmental stages. Briefly, through sociogenesis, or the appropriation of the culturally generated symbolic artifacts that occurs during social interaction, the original biological mental functions are restructured into a higher-order unified psychological system. The system is referred to as higher order because through sociogenesis, we develop the ability to voluntarily control or regulate our psyche. This process of appropriation is captured in the concept of internalization, which can be best understood not as the taking in of something but as the construction of independent verbal and behavioral actions that are functionally equivalent to the actions of social others. As a consequence of the first two processes, our relationship to physical and social reality and to ourselves is mediated, meaning that reality does not directly impact our psychological activity as it does in other species but that it is filtered through the symbolic cultural system. Among other things, this imbues us with the capacity to act through what Vygotsky called 'doubled-experience.' In other words, unlike other animals, whose behavior is a direct reaction to the world, humans can inhibit our reactions in order to first, plan an action before implementing it in the material world. This includes not only producing structures such as buildings designed by architects, but also speech plans for what we want to express to others in social interaction. The final principle states that the process of internalization leading to development is carried out through a sequence in which our mental, and physical, behavior, is at first controlled, or regulated by others, largely through social speech. It then comes under our own control as social speech is eventually directed not at someone else but at the self, as speech takes on a psychological function. Given its social origins, psychological speech is at first external and observable by others. Eventually, however, it evolves into inner speech in its final stage as our psychological processes become internally regulated.

The principles outlined above formed the foundation of a theory of education originally proposed by a psychologist influenced by Vygotsky works, P. Gal'perin, on the assumption that the principles that account for everyday development would also be relevant for the systematically organized development that occurs in educational settings. Gal'perin referred to his approach as Systemic Theoretical Instruction, which he implemented in the schools of Moscow for instruction in virtually all school subjects, including language. However, Gal'perin's understanding of language was largely structurally based, given the influence of theories such as those proposed by Saussure and Bloomfield. Today, there are more useful meaning-based theories of language, such as Cognitive Linguistics and Systemic Functional Linguistics, which resonate far better with the role that Vygotsky assigned to meaning in the formation of the human psyche. Consequently, Concept-Based Language Instruction (C-BLI) adopted by the three authors as their pedagogical approach highlights conceptual meaning rather than structure as the general unit of instruction. The reader will note this in the discussion of C-BLI presented in the second chapter of the book. Despite the modification of Gal'perin's original proposal, C-BLI, as will become apparent in the presentation of the theory in Chapter 2, incorporates the four core principles accounting for development proposed by Vygotsky. Having said this, how each author was able to adapt the theory to meet locally specific needs is most impressive. It exhibits the creativity of the authors as they seamlessly and effectively melded C-BLI with genre-based writing pedagogy without losing the theoretical integrity of either.

In addition to the contribution of the volume to writing pedagogy as well as the general pedagogical literature of sociocultural theory, an especially attractive feature of the book is the concluding section in which the authors ask and answer a series of practical questions that anyone interested in potentially pursuing C-BLI-based writing pedagogy will find informative. The questions address topics such as the identification and definition of pedagogically relevant concepts and how these may be related to genres, and in my view, the most important question that is all too often taken for granted – How does one recognize development? From the C-BLI perspective, as the authors explain, writing development is about not only changing writing performance as evidenced in the ability to independently produce quality texts, but it is also about enriching learners' understanding of the concept of genre and what learners intentionally seek to accomplish through writing. Crucially, as they point out, development is not a linear process, but as described by Vygotsky, it is a revolutionary process that occurs in leaps and bounds and even moves in unanticipated directions.

Writing instructors, program directors, teacher educators, and researchers interested in pedagogical theory will find this book informative, useful, and perhaps in some very positive ways, eye-opening.

James P. Lantolf
Greer Professor Emeritus in Applied Linguistics
The Pennsylvania State University

1 Introduction

What This Book Is About

The main aim of this book is to outline and exemplify the intersection between Concept-Based Language Instruction (C-BLI) and genre-based writing pedagogy (particularly the English for Specific Purposes approach) for empowering student writers to be more agentive, aware, and strategic in their writing. Moving forward, we will refer to this as Concept-Based Genre Writing pedagogy. Our intention is to strike a balance between systematically laying out the theoretical underpinnings of these frameworks and maintaining a practical eye toward other innovative applications, with the understanding that other volumes are entirely dedicated to laying out their principles in detail. We value that both pedagogies strive to be future-oriented and transformational while placing learners' agency and choice at the pedagogical center of teaching and learning.

With this book we target teachers and researchers alike, at any stage in their career working within or interested in working within genre-based and second language writing traditions and/or the C-BLI framework. That is to say that we have novices and experts in one or both traditions in mind, and we endeavor to shape and motivate a framework that integrates them. In this effort, we do not articulate a flaw in work in either tradition, but rather we note the intersections where they exist and the power of working within the two frameworks simultaneously. Importantly, while we foreground and frame writing, we believe that everything in this book also applies to the teaching of language and genre beyond written modalities.

Moving forward, and because much of the writing in the middle of this book is led by a different author presenting their doctoral dissertation work, we refer to ourselves by our surnames: Casal, Kurtz, and Qiu. We serve as *Teacher-Researchers*, which brings teaching and researching on level ground, frames the interdependence of these terms in our work, and practically reflects that each of us was the teacher and researcher in the projects we showcase here. The chapters are not sequenced in author order, but rather in chronological order that the projects were first implemented.

How (and Why) This Book Came to Be

This book emerges from many conversations the three of us shared in 2022 and 2023 in scheming, planning, and preparing for a featured colloquium we presented at the Symposium on Second Language Writing in Tempe, AZ, in October 2023. The response was positive enough to encourage us to keep going, as we recognized that many of our colleagues shared our pedagogical values even while not openly working within this framework. There were many good comments and questions during the conference and after, with plenty of encouragement for more. We enjoyed working together enough to push for keeping the productive conversations going, and it was evident in our talks that there was plenty more to say.

We share the beliefs that all communicative acts resonate with past genre practices at both individual and cultural levels of history, with communicative decisions made by locally weighing conventionality and individual expression. Such decisions are *choices*, and we believe that language and writing pedagogy best prepares learners for such agentive discernment by equipping them with psychological tools for thinking about and engaging with the world abstractly and in weighing factors in dynamic localized activity. Language and writing instruction, even with the best intentions, is often vulnerable to instructional and assessment pressures that prioritize the production of texts (and forms) which *more closely resemble* conventional genre exemplars rather than changes in how learners make decisions and orient toward genre tasks. Likewise, learners themselves are often tempted or pressured to take up example features and constructions as formulas, rather than instantiations of complex, situated sociocognitive contemplation that reflect the social activity of writing, even if such contemplation is momentary.

We argue that writing (and language) pedagogy should be oriented toward particular community genre practices and around systematic concepts that may be taken up by learners as psychological tools for future activity. In this way, genre can be seen as both 'psychological and social' (Hudson, 2007: 206) – or rather a '*frame* for social action' (Bazerman, 1997: 19; emphasis added), with writers carefully navigating dynamic local goals in genre practices through complex cognitive processes. To participate meaningfully in such practices, even for pedagogical purposes, such practices must be meaningful themselves, and learners require a basis from which to intentionally orient to and interact with such tasks. C-BLI and genre-based writing pedagogies frame such goals and pathways, situating teaching and learning around the interactional space that emerges between an educator and a learner and projects toward the learner's future.

Moving back a bit, our broader impetus for bringing our dissertations together was the realization that they were far more connected than we were aware of when we learned of each other's work. We all had training in both an English for Specific Purposes approach to genre theory and C-BLI, as well as broader interest in the work of Vygotsky. Our dissertations individually outlined the implementation of C-BLI and specific-purposes pedagogy. However, while each had pieces of this framework foregrounded and featured, our conversations illuminated a broader picture than we had fully realized on our own. Casal and Kurtz had many years of professional fellowship and discussion regarding domain-specific writing instruction, particularly in Penn State Dickenson Law, where Casal taught legal writing for a semester in a program that Kurtz co-developed and, at the time of this writing, runs. Through these conversations and pedagogical collaborations, they realized that their dissertations, which were defended three years apart from each other, aligned in spirit and theory. While Kurtz conducted a C-BLI intervention in a specific genre context, Casal used C-BLI in an intervention designed around graduate student genre knowledge. In this way, their studies foreground C-BLI and genre-based writing instruction, respectively, but they drew from both traditions. Qiu, who finished his doctoral work four years later, was more directly influenced by Casal's dissertation and collaborations at the time, and his work brings this framework more into balance. He also carries it into a new discipline and includes multiple high-value innovations that demonstrate its potential and vibrancy.

And so, rather than turn our sprawling dissertation projects into the separate books we may at some point each have thought was warranted, we instead convene them here together with the view that doing so gives a more powerful illustration of the value of our framework and a more compelling case for taking it up in your unique project and/or context. Certainly, our most complete articulation of this framework is presented in (and has resulted from) this volume.

Overview of the Book

After this brief introduction (Chapter 1), the book is comprised of eight other chapters. Chapter 2 lays out the theoretical tenets of genre-based writing pedagogies and C-BLI, as well as the important points of intersection that we draw together as a framework. First, it outlines major approaches to genre theory and how they are perhaps less siloed and distinct than once was true. Considerable attention is dedicated to the importance of explicit instructions in many approaches to genre pedagogy, including English for Specific Purposes, which is most closely linked to the work of the authors, but also Systemic Functional Linguistics and Rhetorical Genre Studies. Then an overview of C-BLI is presented, outlining broader components of Vygotskian Sociocultural

Theory including mediated cognition and learning, psychological tools, and the important distinction between scientific and everyday concepts in the work of Vygotsky. This discussion is followed by an explanation of six core phases of a C-BLI pedagogy, as outlined in Poehner and Lantolf (2024): pre-understanding, concept presentation, materialization, verbalization/languaging, performance, and internalization. The chapter concludes with a discussion of the integration of these theoretical and pedagogical frameworks into a Concept-Based Genre Writing pedagogy, with an emphasis on the role of explicit knowledge, the goal of bringing about awareness and agency, the transformational imperative/aim, and the orientation toward participation in real-world activities.

Chapters 3 through 8 form three pairs that each present a large Concept-Based Genre Writing pedagogy. The first chapter in each pair outlines the pedagogical site, learners, target concepts, genre space, and other important methodological and pedagogical considerations. The second chapter in each pair presents an analysis of learner development as an illustration of the framework.

Chapters 3 and 4 present a Concept-Based Genre Writing pedagogy that taught legal analogical reasoning to L2 English speakers in a pre-Master of Laws (LLM) program in the United States, carried out by Kurtz (Kurtz, 2017). Identification of the focal concept occurred through the practical experience of working as a writing specialist in the LLM program and observing students orienting to legal writing through the framework of their prior legal training. Analogical reasoning represents a distinguishing feature of the US legal system compared to the legal systems of the majority of LLM students' home countries. The Concept-Based Genre Writing pedagogy was implemented in a course companion to a Criminal Law course in which the students were enrolled and for which the students would take a final exam comprised of traditional law school questions. Thus, the Concept-Based Genre Writing pedagogy taught the law school exam (IRAC) in addition to the focus on legal analogical reasoning. The development of one focal student, Jun, is tracked across the course of one semester as he engages (or chooses not to engage) with legal analogical reasoning in his IRAC essays. Development is observed both in his ability to reason by analogy in his writing and his ability to discuss his analogical reasoning decisions in instructional conversation with Kurtz.

Chapters 5 and 6 present a Concept-Based Genre Writing pedagogy that taught shell nouns and rhetorical moves (among other features not discussed here) to L2 English doctoral student writers in a cross-disciplinary research writing course, carried out by Casal (Casal, 2020). Student writers represented 12 disciplines across two sections, including humanities, social sciences, and information/technology sciences, and both theoretical and applied physical sciences. Casal selected target concepts based on course needs and published research but also developed course materials through a large corpus-based genre analysis project. During the course, each participant worked with the instructor to compile a personal corpus of published texts within their discipline, and the pedagogy made use of these personal corpora for mediated corpus-based language analysis and discourse-based genre analysis activities as interfacing and mutually informing activities to engage with target concepts in context while grappling with the breadth of their local instantiation. Two participants (pseudonyms Mona and Lucia) are tracked through the term, drawing on audio-recordings of pair work during class activities and text-based stimulated recall interviews with Casal.

Chapters 7 and 8 present a Concept-Based Genre Writing pedagogy project that taught discipline-appropriate sentence-level grammatical features to L1 Chinese students in Mechanical Engineering, carried out by Qiu (Qiu, 2024a, 2024b). Drawing insights from a three-pronged needs analysis at the pre-understanding phase, Qiu identified four key sentence-level linguistic concepts related to effective communication in Mechanical Engineering research article writing, namely, types of clauses, intra-sentence discoursal functions, grammatical stance expressions, and inter-sentence flow and emphasis. During the five-week writing intervention, students were tasked with a scientific presentation of each concept using flowcharts as didactic models, a sentence rewriting activity on teacher-prepared authentic disciplinary writing data, a corpus query activity on a class corpus of research articles in Mechanical Engineering, and a self-exploration activity on their own draft of a for-publication manuscript submitted before the intervention. Students' performance in various in-class text and corpus activities, as well as their interactions with the class corpus, were screen-captured and analyzed. At the end of the intervention, students video-recorded themselves revising their first research writing draft mediated through instructional materials (e.g. the corpus, flowcharts, class handouts). Text- and video-based stimulated recall interviews were then conducted, in which students verbalized their rationale for concept or material selections underlying revision choices. Through different activities and materials, the chapters assess one focal student's (Geyao) developing understanding of grammatical stance expressions at multiple timepoints during the intervention.

Chapter 9, the final chapter of the book, adopts a forward-looking stance. In this chapter, we provide a more direct discussion of important considerations for bringing C-BLI and genre-based language teaching into a real classroom context. We first discuss emerging points of intersection across our interventions with relevance for other contexts. Next, we explicitly turn to the future in a section roughly structured by the six phases of C-BLI outlined in Chapter 2. Here we address considerations such as identifying target scientific concepts and/or genres for the pedagogy, creating concept visualizations and materializations, assessing learners' pre-understandings of concepts, presenting concepts to learners to develop systematic and high-quality understanding of concepts, making activity concrete and practical, and providing responsive mediation to learners.

2 Key Principles and Concepts

Genre-Based Writing Pedagogy

Multiple approaches to genre

Theories of genre are unified in framing genre practices around social contexts and communities, communicative purposes, and expectations and conventions, with the recognition that such practices are dynamic, consequential, and recognizable. Pedagogically speaking, genre-based writing pedagogy encompasses a range of approaches to prepare student writers for agentive participation in genre practices. Theories of genre have evolved significantly since the 1980s, with three major schools of thought* typically identified: the text-first (or linguistic) approaches of English for Specific Purposes (ESP) and Systemic Functional Linguistics (SFL), as well as the context-first approach of Rhetorical Genre Studies (RGS). These schools, while distinct in their origins and initial foci in terms of genre practices, learners, and learning contexts, have increasingly found common ground, particularly in North American university writing contexts. For educators and teachers of multilingual writers, understanding these approaches – and how they can work together – is crucial for developing effective genre-based instruction. Similarly, while our scholarly work is positioned in ESP traditions most directly, our framework draws from textual and contextual philosophies through emphasis on empowering learners to make situational decisions.

The ESP approach, often associated with rhetorical move analysis and the work of John Swales, aims to help both L1 and L2 students succeed in academic and professional contexts (Swales, 1990). More specifically, it targets 'the ability to identify, construct, interpret and successfully exploit a specific repertoire of professional, disciplinary or workplace genres to participate in the daily activities and to achieve the

---

* See, for example, Hyon (1996). Swales (2012) further added two: the Brazilian approach to genre (Araújo et al., 2010; Vian Jr., 2012) and the academic literacies work on student writing carried out in the United Kingdom (Coffin & Donahue, 2012; Flowerdew, 2020; Wingate & Tribble, 2012).

goals of a specific professional community' (Bhatia, 2004: 145). This framework intertwines the concepts of genre, task, and discourse community, all linked by communicative purpose – the shared goals that shape how members of a discourse community use language (Flowerdew, 2015). This approach emphasizes task-based, consciousness-raising activities that focus on authentic real-world texts and encourage students to engage in discussion, critique, and evaluation of rhetorical intentions and phraseology. With a unique task in responding to a growing representation of international students in North American higher education, the ESP approach to genre-based writing can 'short-cut the long processes of situated acquisition' (Hyland, 2007: 151).

ESP researchers place great emphasis on explicit discussions of generic exemplars or instances (i.e. textual forms) in classroom settings, believing that such discussions can lead to students' understanding of both the formal features of genre and the sociorhetorical parameters underlying these features (Cheng, 2005). Therefore, it is essential to acknowledge the notion that genre is not a standalone text, but rather refers to communicative expectations and patterns that emerge and coalesce through repeated social actions around the 'consistency of communicative purpose' (Bhatia, 2004: 22) within community contexts. The ESP approach has been particularly influential in English for Academic Purposes and English for Professional Communication classrooms, where students need to quickly develop control over specialized ways of writing. Scholars in these contexts have proposed that genre-based applications can help non-native speakers of English master the functions and linguistic conventions of texts they need to read and write in their disciplines and professions (Bhatia, 1993; Flowerdew, 1993; Hyland, 2007; Swales, 1990). As will be discussed later, the emphasis on awareness and explicit knowledge resonates with C-BLI.

The Systemic Functional Linguistics (SFL) approach, often referred to as the 'Sydney School,' provides a comprehensive framework for understanding how language creates meaning in context. Grounded in Halliday's work, this approach defines genres as 'staged, goal-oriented purposeful activity' (Martin, 1984: 25). SFL explores how different genres unfold in a 'purposeful, interactive, and sequential' manner (Cheng, 2005), illustrating the connection between language, its function, and the context in which it is used. The SFL approach has developed a distinctive pedagogical model known as the 'teaching-learning cycle,' giving significant attention to text and its social purpose, context, content domain, and language. This cycle, as described by Feez (2002), Feez and Joyce (1998), Hammond *et al.* (1992), and Rothery (1994), consists of three main stages and has some basis in, and resonance with, the work of Vygotsky (see Cheng, 2005): deconstruction (analysis of model texts), joint construction (collaborative text creation), and independent construction of texts (Flowerdew, 2016; Hyon, 1996). At the deconstruction phase, teachers and students analyze model texts together, making explicit how language choices create meaning. The class then moves to joint construction, where they collaboratively create texts in the target genre, with the teacher modeling expert writer decision-making. Finally, in the independent construction phase, students compose their own texts, applying their developing genre knowledge (e.g. Caplan & Farling, 2016; Walsh Marr, 2021). Throughout this cyclic process, there is a strong emphasis on setting context and building field knowledge. Those working within an SFL genre framework theorize continuous interplay between culture, social context, and the purposes, structure, and language of texts. In particular, they have long invested in identifying core genres that shape both general Australian culture and government-supported schools (Cheng, 2005).

The Rhetorical Genre Studies (RGS) approach, also known as the New Rhetoric school, emerged from North American scholarship in rhetoric, composition studies, and professional writing. This approach prioritizes the situational contexts in which genres emerge over their structural or linguistic forms, with a particular focus on the social purposes or actions that genres serve within these contexts (Bazerman, 1988; Devitt, 1993; Freedman & Medwey, 1994; Miller, 1984). Correspondingly, RGS can be said to adopt a less structured pedagogical approach compared to ESP and SFL (Kessler & Polio, 2024). While ESP emphasizes analyzing language patterns and rhetorical moves, and SFL follows the teaching-learning cycle, RGS often prioritizes awareness of how genres function within their social and contextual environments (Freedman, 1999). From this perspective, writing teachers have been more concerned with cultivating first-year university students and novice professionals' awareness of and relationship with genre practices within specific communities, as newcomers become socialized into disciplinary ways of speaking and writing (Berkenkotter & Huckin, 1995). In essence, the goal of writing pedagogy is to enhance students' understanding of all of the 'life' embodied in texts, not just to give them 'the formal trappings of the genres they need to work in' (Bazerman, 1988: 320, as cited in Hyon, 1996).

Explicit instruction and awareness raising in genre-based writing

While explicit language and genre instruction is a fundamental component of pedagogy in the ESP and SFL traditions, historically, the RGS approach has approached explicit genre instruction more cautiously (see Bawarshi & Reiff, 2010; Hyon, 2017). Those researching and teaching within an ESP framework have focused largely on second language or multilingual student writers (often in English-language higher education contexts), long advocating for explicit instruction in genre features. This method, often termed 'metacommunicating' (Flowerdew, 1993;

Swales & Lindemann, 2002, as cited in Paltridge, 2013), involves the explicit analysis of examples of particular genres used in the classroom to heighten learners' awareness of the interconnections between genre-specific language features, rhetorical organization, and communicative purposes (Swales, 1990). Scholars trust that such pedagogy can lead to students' understanding of not only the formal features of genre (e.g. genre-specific lexicogrammar), but also the sociorhetorical factors underlying these formal features (Cheng, 2005), allowing students to respond to different requirements and to analyze existing features within these contexts (Tardy *et al.*, 2020). Furthermore, ESP scholars argue that explicit instruction is particularly beneficial for L2 learners who may be at a disadvantage in unfamiliar naturalistic settings. The SFL approach also incorporates explicit instruction through its teaching-learning cycle (described in Cope & Kalantzis, 1993). SFL demonstrates commitment to explicit instruction particularly to help culturally or socioeconomically disadvantaged students navigate academic life and build textual cultural capital with some confidence (Hammond & Macken-Horarik, 1999).

Some RGS scholars like Bazerman (1988) and Freedman (1993, 1994) questioned the value of explicit genre teaching, suggesting it might even be counterproductive if teachers' understanding of target genres was incomplete. Similarly, recognizing the value of social contexts, Berkenkotter and Huckin (1995) argued that genre knowledge cannot be 'explicitly taught' but is acquired through disciplinary enculturation 'as apprentices become socialized to the ways of speaking [or writing] in particular disciplinary communities' (1995: 7). Wardle (2009) likewise notes that an explicit teaching of academic genres in first-year composition can be problematic since students cannot truly engage in these genres within their authentic rhetorical situations. Relatedly, scholars within the context-first approach have raised questions regarding the focus in ESP and SFL traditions on features of the final product. The RGS tradition has long stressed the significance of viewing writing as a social action and a process embedded in particular contexts. This perspective shifts attention from the written product to the process itself and the social context in which writing takes place, whereas an emphasis on textual features and linguistic patterns tends to prioritize the analysis of finished texts as the locus of activity. It should be noted, as is discussed in Chapter 6 of this volume, that a textual-linguistic approach to genre instruction does run the risk of promoting uncritical replication of textual conventions. Our integrated Concept-Based Genre Writing pedagogy framework usefully bridges this divide and addresses this risk. Our pedagogy emphasizes processes of deciding and meaning making through the acquisition of conceptual resources as psychological tools for thinking about and navigating situated genre practices. It recognizes that genre knowledge develops through active engagement with social contexts, not just through studying genre as 'a text in and of itself' (Tardy & Gevers, 2024), but equipping learners with a concept also provides a basis for orienting to and engaging agentively with writing activity.

And more broadly, despite these apparent differences, there has been a growing recognition of the productivity of integrating insights from all three approaches (e.g. Swales, 2012; Tardy, 2011; Tardy *et al.*, 2020) and an observation that many practitioners blend aspects of these genre *theories* in pedagogical practice (Kessler & Casal, 2024). This convergence is driven by their considerable overlap in theorizing community, purpose, and practice as pillars of genre and in setting agentive participation in community genre practices as the pedagogical goal. Swales (2011) observes that 'these so-called "three traditions" have, fifteen years later, largely coalesced, particularly in terms of practical and pedagogical applications' (2011: 85). He notes that scholars such as Johns (1997) and Devitt (2004) have successfully leveraged the strengths of more than one tradition in their work to meet student needs. Likewise, scholars primarily associated with the RGS approach, such as Artemeva and Freedman (2016), similarly find a productivity drawing ESP and RGS together in research and pedagogy. Johns (2011) suggests that curricula should begin with texts and their structures (as in ESP and SFL approaches) but then move toward an integration of theories and practices that value analysis of context, complex writing processes, and intertextuality. This integrated approach helps students understand texts as both 'temporarily structured and evolving,' drawing from established conventions while remaining responsive to new situations (Johns, 2011).

From another perspective, Tardy *et al.* (2020) and Tardy and Gevers (2024) argue that the distinction between teaching for genre acquisition (often associated with ESP and SFL approaches) and genre awareness (more commonly linked to RGS) may be somewhat artificial. As multilingual writers navigate unfamiliar academic and professional contexts in a new language, the dual focus on acquisition and awareness helps them develop 'rhetorical flexibility' – the ability to understand and adapt genre conventions across different contexts (Tardy *et al.*, 2020: 292). Bawarshi and Reiff (2010) highlight the common ground shared by these approaches, noting that 'both linguistic and rhetorical approaches to genre – whether in the form of Systemic Functional Linguistics, English for Specific Purposes, or Rhetorical Genre Studies – share a fundamental understanding of genre as inextricably tied to situation' (2010: 57). Theorization of situational practices is a point of high contact between genre theories and C-BLI, which aims to equip learners with psychological tools not for arriving at 'correct' target answers, but for locally weighing contextual factors of situations, expectations, and carefully calibrated personal intentions.

Our discussion highlights that these orientations agree on several general characteristics of genre. First, the goal of genre-based instruction is to develop awareness of genre as a conceptual frame for thinking about real-world practices, with a gradual reduction in the historical divide between the context-first approach and text-first ones (Tardy *et al.*, 2020). Increased genre awareness in turn supports genre-specific knowledge development (Negretti & McGrath, 2018), which may include contextual, linguistic, or rhetorical aspects of a community genre practice. Second, all approaches recognize that writers make deliberate choices within genre constraints when writing in their disciplines and professions, emphasizing writer agency in genre production. Third, there is a shared emphasis on the importance of engaging with real-world verbal and textual interactions in the target domain. This view allows for a comprehensive approach to genre pedagogy, one that equips students with tools, frames, and experiences to become agentive members of discourse communities. The goal is not simply to produce texts that look more like targets, but to develop a toolkit for thinking about engaging in genre practices.

A more integrated approach to genre theory helps writing teachers avoid two potential pitfalls: reducing genre instruction to formula-following or leaving students to struggle without explicit guidance. This approach aims to develop both genre-specific knowledge and broader genre awareness, recognizing that understanding the process and context of writing is just as important as understanding the expectations and mastering the formal features of specific genres. It cultivates a relationship with writing that goes beyond producing textual products that conform to certain conventions, encouraging students to see writing as a way of participating in and shaping discourse communities, while also developing the tools to do so. C-BLI provides a robust means of theorizing and provoking such development.

Concept-Based Language Instruction

The mediated mind and psychological tools

Each of the three studies reported on in this book frames writing instruction through an integrated approach to genre theory and also relies on a theory of learning derived from Vygotskian's sociocultural theory (V-SCT). For the present purposes, we focus on three core concepts in V-SCT that drive meaning-making potential in C-BLI. This section first briefly discusses those key concepts – mediation, psychological tools, and conceptual knowledge – before discussing C-BLI.

Mediation is 'the central concept of sociocultural theory' (Lantolf & Thorne, 2006: 59). In V-SCT, humans are understood not to act on the world directly, but instead through tools which human cultures have created and use to accomplish tasks in the world. These tools 'mediate and regulate our relationships with others and with ourselves and thus change the nature of these relationships' (Lantolf, 2000: 1), affecting the ongoing cognitive development of individuals within a society. The tools that mediate an individual's interaction with the world are both material and psychological. This is because in V-SCT, humans are understood to inhabit two worlds – one material, that is, physical objects, and one 'comprised of signs and symbols, managed primarily through language' (Lantolf & Thorne, 2006: 59). Both of these worlds precede an individual human and affect development, from infancy to adulthood and from novice to expert.

Returning to the nature of tools, both material and psychological tools are culturally imbued. Material tools (e.g. silverware, rakes, pencils) are physical objects human cultures created to act on the environment. These tools are cultural in that they were created by humans for a particular purpose (e.g. spreading butter with a butter knife) and passed onto future generations. For example, the utensils conventionally used in cultures vary throughout the world; these tools exist in the culture and need not be recreated by each generation. Material tools were created for a particular purpose but also can be used for novel, unintended purposes (e.g. using a butter knife as a screwdriver) (Lantolf & Poehner, 2014: 8). As discussed below, one of the phases of C-BLI involves development and use of tools that make the concept under study *material* in some way to the students. This may be a physical, material object, as in Serrano-Lopez and Poehner (2008) where students manipulated clay objects to conceptualize Spanish prepositions, or the concepts may be materialized in that a holistic depiction of the concept is made visible to students through a teaching aid such as a drawing, flowchart, or map.

Throughout, we refer to material(ized) mediation and social mediation. In teaching multilingual writers, much of the work instructors do is already in the sphere of cultural artifacts as psychological tools, rather than material tools. Certainly, the material tools used in writing – pencil and paper or computer – matter, but our focus in the book and in our studies is on guiding students to appropriate new cultural artifacts meaningfully. To do so, we often materialize – or make the psychological visual – genres and concepts being studied. As such, the material(ized) mediation we refer to are didactic models and teaching tools that guide novice writers and help them make decisions when writing in genres they are gaining control over. Whether physical objects, such as Cuissenaire rods for understanding story grammar of L2 narratives (Buescher, 2015), or a visualized representation such as a flowchart as Qiu used in his study (see Chapter 7), these teaching tools make conceptual knowledge visible externally and accessible to the learner for reference, discussion, and use.

Like material tools, psychological tools are also culture-specific, passed through generations, and necessary for individuals to function within society. These psychological tools are understood to be 'those symbolic systems specific for a given culture that when internalized by individualized learners become their inner cognitive tools' (Kozulin, 2005: 3), which represent powerful means of mediation for humans.

Examples of these tools, which can be used to regulate our physical or mental behavior, include music, maps, numbers, and art. According to V-SCT, the 'most pervasive and powerful of human symbolic creations is language,' so much so that it is language 'as the quintessential human signification system, that Vygotsky situated at the heart of his psychological theory' (Lantolf & Poehner, 2014: 9). While material tools allow humans to act on the world, psychological tools allow humans to regulate and act on ourselves. That is, psychological tools, chief among them language, may also be inwardly directed with the goal of self-regulation (Vygotsky, 1978: 55).

The social mediation offered to students in the course of internalizing a concept is also central to the studies presented in this volume. In V-SCT, social mediation refers to activity engaged in with a more capable other (often, the teacher) and the cues, hints, and feedback that the more capable other gives to the student(s) to first diagnose incomplete understanding or misunderstanding and then to guide them to more complete understanding of the concept. The three teacher-researchers in the studies outlined in the book adopt the role of a mediator who dynamically participates in goal-directed pedagogical activity with assistance attuned to student utterances, understandings, and orientations. When engaged in this goal-directed activity, a mediator attends to the psychological, regulatory function of speech. That is, language is a psychological tool that allows human beings to regulate their own behavior, their interactions with others, and ultimately the material world. A mediator attends to this powerful function of language to guide the student to internalization of the concept so that the concept is available for such psychological regulation.

These interactions can be conceptualized through Vygotsky's concept of the Zone of Proximal Development, a metaphorical, emergent arena for collaborative activity where expert-others and learners accomplish 'through collaborative mediation what is unachievable alone' (Lantolf, 2011a: 29) for the learner. Collaborative mediation encompasses social mediation provided by the expert-other, responsivity on the part of the learner, and conceptual mediation designed to be used as a psychological tool. Importantly, engaging in Zone of Proximal Development activity and providing mediation is different from providing corrective feedback. From the perspective of V-SCT, the goal of mediation 'is not to correct learner language per se, but to promote learner development through provision of hints, cues, leading questions, including explicit information when necessary, on how to appropriately formulate specific features of the L2' (Lantolf *et al.*, 2017: 154). Rather, the goal of mediation is to guide the learner toward independent, self-regulated performance (Poehner, 2008b). The Zone of Proximal Development thus provides a means of internalization and assessment simultaneously.

This is what Vygotsky means when he describes development as appearing twice: first, on the social level, or interpsychologically 'between' people, and then 'inside' an individual, or intrapsychologically (Vygotsky, 1978: 57). In the multilingual writing contexts discussed in this book, we encounter novices developing control over specific features within genres important for their futures. First, discussion of the feature occurs on the social level. The feature or genre is discussed in class, perhaps examples of the genre are read and discussed. Initial student attempts at the genre or feature are discussed. Much of this occurs on the intermental plane. Through social activity with the teacher and classmates, the learner develops understanding of and control over this new feature. Eventually, the student will not need to rely on others or on material(ized) mediation to produce the feature or genre appropriately. It has become intramental.

Related to Vygotsky's understanding of the *mediated mind* and *psychological tools* are his writings on the development of conceptual knowledge and his interest in formal education. Concepts are understood to be cultural as '[h]uman cultures create categories for organizing events and objects in the world' (Lantolf & Poehner, 2014: 9). Vygotsky distinguished between *everyday concepts* (also called *spontaneous*) and *scientific concepts*, a distinction with direct relevance for educational activity. Everyday concepts originate from experience in the world, are inductively formed and empirical, require a long period of development, and their internalization results in unsystematic and often incomplete knowledge. Everyday concepts arise through experience in the everyday world and are loosely organized meanings resulting from the activity of daily life; this creates an incredibly sense-laden and powerful way to understand the world, but they are often erroneous (e.g. whales are fish; the sun rises) or incomplete (e.g. flowers grow because it rains; cold temperatures cause colds).

Conversely, *scientific concepts* are abstract, systematic, generalizable, and theoretical; scientific concepts reveal the essential quality of an entity or process (Lantolf & Poehner, 2014: 61). Unlike everyday concepts, scientific concepts are available to conscious reflection and Vygotsky argues that they should comprise the basic unit of instruction in properly organized education. For example, in school, students learn that the earth rotates around the sun (scientific concept), rather than the sun rises in the East and sets in the West as perception of the everyday world would lead us to believe (everyday concept).

According to V-SCT, the two types of concepts form a dialectical unity, and both allow humans to function in society. The strength of one is the weakness of the other. Everyday concepts are open to spontaneous usage, and application to various concrete solutions; they are developed with the richness of empirical content and saturated with personal experience, but this empirical development results in their being tied to concrete situations, and not sufficiently abstract to be flexible and not directly accessible to consciousness (Vygotsky, 1987: 218). Scientific concepts are inherently more abstract and open to conscious reflection that allows for intentional and volitional use, greater flexibility and control by the individual. They lack, however, the richness of personal experience of everyday concepts; the internalization of abstract academic concepts must be linked to practical, goal-oriented activity.

The phases of concept-based language instruction

These core concepts (mediation, psychological tools, and conceptual knowledge) underpin the development of C-BLI pedagogies. In C-BLI, the basic unit of instruction is the scientific concept. Teachers explain concepts to students, often through the aid of visual didactic materials, and guide the students in goal-oriented practical activity so that students appropriate the concept for use in subsequent goal-oriented activity. Critical to C-BLI is that the teachers' explanation systematically presents students with conceptual knowledge prior to guiding them through purposeful activities that require use of the conceptual knowledge in practical activity. Internalization is understood to be achieved when students have developed the ability to use the concept as a psychological tool in activity (Lantolf, 2011b). That is, when students are able to use the academic concept under study as a psychological tool to mediate their practical, application-based activity, the concept is understood to be internalized. The phases of C-BLI are: orientation/pre-understanding, concept presentation, materialization, verbalization/languaging, performance, and internalization (Poehner & Lantolf, 2024).

The orientation or pre-understanding (Miller, 2011) phase meets students where they are, or rather, it locates them. This phase, which can also be called the Orienting Basis of Action (OBA), is where current understanding of students is established so that an instructional plan can be made. This phase is critical because 'it informs the teacher and makes the students aware of what they know or think they know about a language feature and how they use it to plan and carry out communicative action' (Poehner & Lantolf, 2024: 20). For teachers of multilingual writers, establishing students' pre-understanding gives insight into the extent to which students are orienting to a genre using scientific concepts from their home culture that differ or are perhaps using spontaneous concepts. The diagnosis of pre-understanding will shape the subsequent phases. For example, in Kurtz's study (see Chapters 3 and 4), students were engaged in a problem-solving activity in order to understand their orientation to legal writing as lawyers in their home countries and this activity also revealed spontaneous concepts related to their pre-course understanding of US legal writing. In Casal's study (see Chapters 5 and 6), learners oriented to academic writing broadly through grammar-based rules of thumb and everyday understandings of target concepts.

The second phase of C-BLI, the concept presentation phase, provides a coherent and complete definition of the academic concept to learners. As discussed above, scientific concepts are developed through formal education and are 'generalizations of the experience of humankind that are fixed in science, understood in the broadest sense of the term to include both natural and social science as well as the humanities' (Karpov, 2003: 71). That is, scientific concepts are holistic, generalizable, and represent the fruits of scientific inquiry. In C-BLI, 'the concept must focus on the meaning of each feature rather than its structure' (Poehner & Lantolf, 2024: 20). Thus, studies in C-BLI have historically looked to meaning-based rather than structure-based linguistic theories to provide the theoretical explanations used in C-BLI. This is also why we propose that with its focus on students agentively making meaning-based decisions about their writing, genre-based pedagogy is a powerful partner for C-BLI in teaching multilingual writers.

At the concept presentation phase, it is important for students to understand the concept, but rote memorization is not the goal. Rote memorization of definitions does not lead to the ability to use that knowledge dynamically in a practical, goal-based activity, and students making agentive decisions in a subsequent goal-based activity is the goal of a C-BLI program. For example, Qiu explains in Chapter 7 how he first identified linguistic concepts important for engineering communication and then how he used theoretical understanding of those concepts from linguistics to provide explanations to students.

During the materialization phase, 'the teacher presents students with a visual representation of the concept explained in phase 2' (Poehner & Lantolf, 2024: 22). In C-BLI, such visual representations are called Schema for Complete Orienting Basis of an Action (SCOBA). Recall that in the first phase, the pre-understanding phase, the purpose was to uncover students' pre-understanding. That is, in the first phase teachers learn how students already orient to the concept under study. In the materialization phase, through the aid of SCOBAs, teachers begin the process of reshaping that understanding, that basis of action. A SCOBA is intended to represent the concept under study holistically and visually so that students can use it in goal-directed activity during course activities.

SCOBAs are critical to a C-BLI program because the focus in C-BLI is not on students memorizing definitions of concepts. Rather, the heart of C-BLI is that students internalize a concept for flexible use in future, goal-directed activities. SCOBAs are useful in achieving this goal because, by their very nature as visual representations, they avoid any tendency toward memorization. As an external and material(ized) tool, SCOBAs can be referred to in goal-directed activity until students are able to use the concept as a psychological tool without such external assistance.

The SCOBAs represented in the studies discussed in this book demonstrate that there is no one way to develop a SCOBA. So long as SCOBAs represent the concept holistically and are made available as an external aid for students to use in goal-directed activity, they may be appropriate for guiding students to internalizing the academic concept. For example, the SCOBAs used in the studies here varied from picture-based problem-solving activities (Kurtz, Chapter 3) to flowcharts carefully chosen to cater to engineering students' familiarity with diagrammatic learning (Qiu, Chapter 7).

During the next phase, languaging, students are pushed to verbalize their understanding of the concept and its use in goal-directed activity. While the materialization phase by its very nature relies on an external tool to engage students in goal-directed activity, the languaging phase 'begins to move students away from reliance on the external SCOBA and toward a reliance on themselves when carrying out an action' (Poehner & Lantolf, 2024: 25). In the movement away from external tools inward to a reliance on the self, this phase leverages the self-regulatory function of language, as discussed above. This movement inward is typically carried out in two sub-phases, the communicative sub-phase and the dialogic sub-phase.

In the communicative sub-phase, a student is tasked with making their understanding of the concept comprehensible to someone else. This sub-phase highlights the social nature of language and human cognition – explaining the concept to another so that it is comprehensible. However, and critically for the learner's development, it performs a psychological role as the learner's understanding of the concept is also made clear to them. This psychological aspect of the communicative sub-phase pushes the learner toward the second sub-phase, the dialogic phase. For example, in his study, Casal met with students in writing conferences to discuss drafts of research articles and how students used focal concepts (e.g. shell nouns) in their texts. In these conferences, students were encouraged to verbalize their understanding of the focal concepts and how they made decisions about using the concepts in their writing. Casal used these student verbalizations to attune to students' individualized movement toward internalization of the concepts.

In the dialogic sub-phase, the learner communicates with the self about their understanding of the concept and its use in goal-directed activity. This may begin as fully fleshed-out explanations to the self, but gradually will become more abbreviated self-talk, such as short utterances or gestures to help regulate the self. Frawley (1997) notes that 'private speech serves cognition by bringing into focus those features that the person sees as relevant to a particular problem' (as cited in Lantolf & Thorne, 2006: 93). The bringing into focus of what a person sees as relevant to a particular problem has important consequences not just for the learner in her journey of internalization, but also for teachers as mediators. What a student orients to as important is critical for a mediator to understand so that the teacher can provide appropriate cues, feedback, and mediation. For this reason, the power of both the communicative and dialogic sub-phase should not be underestimated in C-BLI.

Due to the data collection methods used in each of the three studies described in this book, we do not analyze robust dialogic languaging. Such self-mediation is possible to observe in, for example, student private writing as they plan their exam essay in Kurtz's study, student self-talk as they make corpus inquiries in Casal's study, or student mouse movements in screen captures of the revision process in Qiu's study.

In the performance phase, students are tasked with *doing*. That is, learners must actually engage in practical, application-based activity where they use their conceptual knowledge to make decisions about meaning-making. In the studies discussed in this book, the performance phase entailed writing in the genres under study over a period of time.

Crucially, this phase helps to avoid what Vygotsky called *verbalism*, an overreliance on scientific knowledge without grounding in concrete activity. That is, from a V-SCT perspective, students must use the concepts under study, not merely repeat definitions or talk about them. Early on in the performance phase, learners will likely rely on external tools to aid their performance. Those external tools may be the SCOBA(s) developed to support their use of a concept, or social mediation in the form of languaging from the teacher or a peer. These forms of mediation or attuned assistance are understood as necessary in C-BLI and learners can and should use them so long as they are necessary. Gradually, however, as students 'gain experience manipulating a particular concept or set of concepts, they are expected to decrease their reliance on the overt manifestation of SCOBAs' (Poehner & Lantolf, 2024: 28) or other mediation.

Finally, the goal of C-BLI is internalization of the concept so that students can use the concept in goal-directed activity without reliance on external aids. In this phase, students can access the meaning of concepts reliably and quickly in order to accomplish goals in their communicative activities. Put in terms of the studies discussed in the following chapters, in Casal's study, conceptual understanding of shell nouns is necessary, but the desired outcome is for students to effectively use such nouns in their writing to build cohesion and frame concepts intentionally. For Qiu's students, it is important that students conceptually understand clausal types and various discoursal functions that they accomplish, but the goal of the intervention is for learners to agentively use discipline-appropriate sentence-level linguistic knowledge in the writing of mechanical engineering research articles.

We must note that while we discuss C-BLI in a sequence of phases, it is not a stepwise procedure where one phase is introduced and then abandoned once 'achieved.' Put another way, C-BLI is discussed in terms of phases for descriptive ease, but should not be considered a linear process where step 1 must be completed before moving on to step 2 and never returned to. Rather, the developmental process in C-BLI is understood to be iterative and fluid and students will return to prior phases for material mediation (SCOBAs) or social mediation (languaging) over time and as necessary. The fluidity of movement through the phases is especially important to the three studies reported on in this book. Each study takes place in the context of writing instruction, where there is often fluid movement between concept presentation, performance (writing) and languaging (feedback, consultation with students about what they intend to communicate and how they can agentively make linguistic decisions that match their intended meaning).

A Concept-Based Genre Writing Pedagogy Framework

Metaphorically speaking, we conceptualize genre-based writing pedagogy as framing the arenas on which student writers aim to perform and C-BLI as a means of equipping them with psychological tools that enable self-regulated, agentive engagement. Genres frame situations characterized by community, purpose, and expectations or conventions, while concepts empower individuals to dynamically weigh local factors in situated decision-making. Through the point of contact of the *situation*, a Concept-Based Genre Writing pedagogy empowers learners to appropriate conceptual tools – framed by the genre practices of their imagined future – as flexible resources for thinking about and engaging with such practices. We define the integration of these two pedagogies on the following premises:

A Concept-Based Genre Writing pedagogy is transformationally projected toward the future. In both genre-based writing pedagogy and C-BLI, the aim is to reorient student writers toward and empower them for participation in genre-practices beyond immediate pedagogical boundaries. This entails internalizing concepts as 'inner cognitive tools' (Kozulin, 2005: 5) that enable new ways of thinking about genre-practices, increasing intentionality, raising awareness, and empowering complex metacognitive reflection. A Concept-Based Genre Writing pedagogy does not merely equip learners with new words to accomplish familiar goals, but rather new ways of thinking about and strategically navigating communicative decision-making and literacy. Internalized concepts are psychological tools, but their application occurs in the concrete activity of reading and writing.

In a Concept-Based Genre Writing pedagogy, learner agency is the goal of development and is evidence of development. Throughout the pedagogy and as the ideal outcome, intentional and agentive decision-making is the target. Internalization of a concept is not merely a matter of 'taking in,' but rather an appropriative acquisition of a new psychological resource that affords new potentials and perspectives. That is, learners acquire concepts for and demonstrate conceptual internalization by their intentional, principled use in concrete, practical activity. Equipped with new psychological tools, learners may make similar decisions for more articulable reasons, may choose to resist genre conventions, may choose to balance their voice with their understanding of genre expectations, or may make entirely creative and unanticipated choices.

A Concept-Based Genre Writing pedagogy targets locally responsive decision-making. While some genre-based writing pedagogy run the risk of perpetuating the conventions of globally powerful language varieties through emphasis on convention, and while learners may be tempted to take up forms for non-critical use in their writing, a Concept-Based Genre Writing pedagogy does not value the production of more target-like texts *per se*. As Van Compernolle *et al.* (2016) explain in a different context, we are not teaching the definitions of concepts or forms 'but rather how particular meanings can be created . . . through the choice of linguistic forms' as well as 'in what circumstances the demands of one category of meaning may outweigh the demands of another' (2016: 343). Thus, while explicit instruction and explicit knowledge play essential roles in our pedagogy, it is to bring about conceptual understandings for flexible local decision-making, rather than reproduction of rules of common forms.

In this spirit, we present pedagogical case studies of learners internalizing analogical reasoning to engage in written genres of law school (Chapters 3 and 4); shell nouns and rhetorical moves to engage in discipline-specific research article writing practices (Chapters 5 and 6); and grammatical stance expressions at the sentence level to engage in research article writing in engineering (Chapters 7 and 8).

3 Legal Writing: Context and Pedagogy

Chapters 3 and 4 present Kurtz's (second author) implementation of Concept-Based Language Instruction (C-BLI) in a legal writing context. The C-BLI course taught analogical reasoning in writing law school exam essays (IRAC essay) to international Master of Laws (LLM) students at a US law school. LLM students overwhelmingly have legal training in countries that follow some version of a civil law system, where the legal case is not a primary source of law. By contrast, in the United States, not only is the legal case a source of primary law, but it is also the premiere teaching tool of legal education. Thus, both culturally and professionally, students need to be oriented to reasoning and writing using legal cases as legal authority. Additionally, while some practitioner-oriented genres are explicitly taught in law school, the pedagogical genre of the IRAC essay, despite its importance to demonstrating learning in law school, is usually not taught explicitly.

Legal Systems as Languacultures

Prior educational and professional history impacts how and what students learn in the L2 writing classroom. The L2 legal classroom embodies this quite robustly. The overwhelming majority of international students in US law schools matriculate in one-year Master of Laws (LLM) programs, which generally require a first, professional law degree or eligibility for entry into legal practice in their home countries. Such students seek an LLM for myriad reasons, but often because an LLM offers a pathway to legal practice in the United States or advancement in their legal career in their home countries. This is to say, LLM students are not legal novices; they are legal professionals with routinized ways of reasoning with and writing about the law.

These routinized ways of legal thinking are not left at the classroom door, because they represent the language, culture, and professional experience of LLM students. Silver (2005) notes, 'Law is uniquely local – it embodies local customs and legitimizes local moral judgments' (p. 2). The understanding of law with which students enter the US legal classroom is imbued with that local understanding – with its local categories and moral judgments. Concurrently, international LLM students are taking on learning a new system entirely, with its rhetorical preferences, specialized language, and local moral judgments. 'Although at first, it seems that their being non-native speakers of English was the most salient feature of this group of students, it became clear to me that their unfamiliarity with the English language was much less problematic than their unfamiliarity with our federal common law legal system and the conventions of U.S. Legal Discourse' (Hoffman, 2011: 2).

Given the culturally imbued nature of law, understanding the study of law in a new context might be usefully thought of as studying a *legal languaculture*. 'Languaculture' conceptualizes language and culture as an indivisible whole (Agar, 2002). Through languaculture, Agar suggests that 'whenever you hear the word *language* or the word *culture,* you might wonder about the missing half' (2002: 60). In short, languaculture is an acknowledgment that language *use* is more than the formal properties of language. The linguistic choices speakers and writers make to shape meaning is always informed by past and local knowledge. As true as this is of everyday language use, it may also be true in the case of a professional domain such as law, perhaps especially the professional domain of law.

To recognize a *legal languaculture*, then, is to understand that knowledge of the different sources of law legal systems recognize, interpretation of those sources of law, how sources of law interact, and the rhetorical preferences of members of the macro languaculture affect what it means to 'think like a lawyer' in different legal systems. This should be taken into consideration when teaching international LLM students because learning how to interpret US common law texts and write for US common law readers requires complex interplay of understanding the legal concepts and how to use language to shape the discourse in a meaningful way for the legal reader.

LLM students enter the US law school classroom as legal reasoners and legal writers with entrenched practices from their prior legal training. That is to say, they enter the US law school classroom with internalized legal languacultures and thus orient to what law is and how to reason with and write about it differently than assumptions made by US legal education. So that differences between the legal languacultures and entrenched ways of thinking may be clearer to the reader, US common law and civil legal systems are briefly described below. Islamic law is not described here, solely because the data analysis chapter focuses on a student trained in civil law and how he engages with the differences between civil and common law written analysis. The development of three students trained in Islamic law is described in Kurtz (2017).

A defining difference between civil and common law systems is whether the decisions of judges – called judicial opinions or legal cases

– are a source of binding law. Civil law systems rely on a codified system of law. A defining characteristic of civil law systems is 'the preeminence of the "codes" over caselaw and legal scholars over the judiciary' (Daly, 1998: 39). In civil law countries such as Germany, France, and Colombia, a historic expectation is that the existing framework of codified law will be sufficient to answer a legal question. Thus, in contrast to the kind of statutory law that US readers may be familiar with, codes in civil law countries tend to be 'both comprehensive and systematic, and typically are enacted at one time' (Thornton, 2014: 16). Thus, 'legal analysis takes the form of application and interpretation of the established rules' (Whalen-Bridge, 2008: 367). Legal actors may consult other, secondary sources of law, such as scholarly interpretations of the law or even reports of judicial decisions, but in a civil law system the code is the primary source of law, and this has implications for the role of courts. While, in common law systems, judicial opinions are a source of law binding on future cases, 'civilian law historically has started from a position that judges are not empowered to create and change the law enacted by the legislature but rather are to read and apply the existing law to new cases' (Murray, 2011: 140).

The United States is a common law system, a type of legal system characterized by the reliance on prior judgments as a primary source of law. Lee *et al.* (2007: 11) write: '[l]aw students and lawyers from non-Anglo-American countries will learn that Anglo-American law is "case law" or "judge-made" law'. Case law being a primary source of law means that prior judgments – decisions in real legal cases – shape the law. The historical assumption in common law is that gaps in the law exist and the law is developed through minute accretion case by case (Whalen-Bridge, 2008). As such, prior judgments become binding on lower courts within the same jurisdiction, setting precedent through the theory of *stare decisis*, 'the doctrine of precedent, under which a court must follow earlier judicial decisions when the same points arise again in litigation' (Garner & Black, 2019: 1696). Thus, for legal reasoners in a common law system, it is necessary to analyze precedent cases to understand what the law is and how to apply it. American attorneys are educated to recognize that they have not thoroughly researched a legal problem if they have not analyzed applicable case law. In fact, '[w]ithout locating and reading the cases that explain the application of the statute or constitutional provision, [US attorneys] have not even begun their research' (Lee *et al.*, 2007: 11). Learning to reason within the US legal system, then, involves learning to interpret both statutes and case law, and reasoning with case law to predict how a case or set of cases might be similar to or different from a case at hand.

As the discussion of civil and common law systems pointed out, a distinguishing difference between the legal languacultures is the status of the judicial opinion as binding law. In the terminology of languacultures, this difference represents a *rich point*. A *rich point* is made visible when two languacultures come into contact and differences between *mine* and *yours* are apparent (Agar, 2002). Through vivid metaphor, Agar describes rich points as different interpretations of what is expected, or possible, in the world:

> When two languacultures come into contact, *yours* and *theirs*, the most interesting problems, the ones that attract your attention, are the vertical cliffs. These cliffs are difficult because – on one side of the barrier or another, or perhaps on both sides – the problematic bit of language is puttied thickly into far-reaching networks of association and many situations of use. When one grabs such a piece of language, the putty is so thick and so spread out that it's almost impossible to lift the piece of language out. (2002: 99–100).

Rich points are where languaculture action is, where the most pronounced differences are apparent. While rich points may make penetration of the target languaculture difficult, they are also where well-organized explicit instruction can make a crucial impact.

In thinking of legal systems as legal languacultures, rich points are a compelling place to target explicit, meaning-focused instruction. Concepts such as *stare decisis* and analogical reasoning, which structure discourse across legal genres, represent quintessential differences in the respective legal cultures. Given these differences it is not surprising that moving from one legal system to another entails a profound cognitive switch and thus analogical reasoning appears to be a rich point, between US law and the legal languacultures LLM students are trained in. In fact, in the context of Legal Writing courses, studies have found some international LLM students engaged in extensive work to bypass the need to reason analogically (Hartig, 2017) or relied on 'common sense' rather than legal arguments in constructing their analogies (Abbuhl, 2005), providing support for the suggestion that while analogical reasoning is a threshold concept for understanding US common law, LLM students may require explicit instruction to develop systematic understanding of legal analogical reasoning.

Legal Analogical Reasoning: A Definition

Recognizing analogical reasoning as a rich point between legal languacultures, it becomes important to define *legal* analogical reasoning. Legal analogical reasoning is not simply comparisons of similarity of appearance. Legal analogies are imbued through the (cultural) categories of law. As Winter (2001: 229) explains, '[e]verything may be like everything else in an infinite number of ways, but *analogy* consists in a mapping that characterizes a *conceptual relation* between domains initially understood as separate'. A legal analogy is 'a conceptual mapping (whether of attributes or relations) that highlights connections that are otherwise not well established in our conceptual system' (Winter, 2001: 237). Cognitively, this mapping is the same process as metaphor; that is, mapping what is known about one (source) domain onto an unknown (target) domain so that one may understand more about the target domain. In legal analogical reasoning, prior legal cases comprise the source domain and a client case or hypothetical comprise the target domain.

Judicial reasoning through legal categories provides the backbone for the conceptual relation in legal analogical reasoning. That is, analogical reasoning for common law analysis is not similarity of narrative stories. It is a mapping of specifically legal similarity, similarities not immediately obvious in our conceptual system, but necessary because of reliance on precedent in a common law system. Legal cases do not merely recount stories of human conflict, they do so 'using categories internal to a legal worldview' (Mertz, 2007: 64) and along lines developed by other cases. For example, the similarities of a loaded gun, a Presa Canario dog, and a hypodermic needle used by a drug addict to inject heroin are not likely to be well established in the reader's mind. That is, in everyday thinking, the similarities are not immediately obvious and available for analogical reasoning because the objects do not physically resemble each other, functionally do not serve the same purpose, and likely have not been connected by our perceptual systems before. The ability to make connections between the three objects, however, is exactly the sort of thinking required by legal analogical reasoning as a scientific concept, and precisely an analogy the focal student of the next chapter, Jun, will make in his development as a legal analogical reasoner.

Based on Winter's (2001) definition of analogy, a framework for identifying *legal analogical reasoning* in student writing was developed. To be *legal analogical reasoning*, an analogy must (1) demonstrate that the legal concept or category is the impetus for making the analogy; (2) make reference to a relevant precedent case fact; (3) compare the precedent case fact to an instant case fact; and (4) convey the relationship between precedent and instant case facts through 'signal language.' Here, signal language refers to sentence structure and word choice that explicitly mark the relationship between the precedent case and the case under analysis.

US Legal Education: A Languaculture

LLM students must orient not only to the new legal languaculture of US common law, but also the cultural and linguistic norms of US legal education. Two cultural norms relevant to this study are the case method, and a single exam or paper constituting the basis for grades. As the second cultural norm implicates the genre taught in the present study, it is discussed more fully than the first.

The case method is teaching law through appellate judicial opinions because these texts are believed to exemplify the reasoning process in US common law. In course casebooks, judicial opinions are presented in excerpted but original form. That is, law students read authentic judicial opinions that have been redacted to teach about a specific legal concept. Typically, the judicial opinion first provides a narration of the human conflict leading to the legal dispute, called the facts in law school and legal discourse. The facts are typically followed by a statement of the legal issue(s) and applicable legal rule(s). Next follows the rationale for the court's decision – an exposition of the reasoning the court used to reach the ruling. Discussion and application of prior case law through analogical reasoning are prominent in the rationale section. As legal cases have been written for a legal audience, the structure, syntax, and vocabulary are notoriously challenging for beginning law students. So, too, is learning to read these technical legal documents as 'conflict stories' constantly filtered 'through the lens of legal-textual authority' (Mertz, 2007: 94).

Historically, law school courses were graded based on a single exam. That exam typically presented students with a single or series of hypothetical fact patterns and required them to write an essay analyzing the relevant legal issue(s), predicting a legal conclusion based on their analysis. This assessment method is still common in US legal education, whether the exam is partly or entirely based on essays. Despite its use as the primary basis for evaluating student performance, the law exam essay receives little pedagogical and scholarly attention. While law schools have Legal Writing courses that teach practitioner-focused genres, it appears no law school teaches a course on writing legal analysis in an exam setting. In fact, some scholars claim many 'law students are never taught how to demonstrate their legal knowledge in an exam scenario' (Strong & Desnoyer, 2016: 3). Put another way, doctrinal courses (e.g. Criminal Law or Torts) teach how to understand legal rules and cases and how to present both sides of an issue orally; legal research and writing classes teach how to use cases and citation, how to structure and write an office memorandum; but doctrinal final exams assess based on the structure of an exam essay and analysis of both sides of an issue in writing, something that is not taught (Haverstick, 2024: 162).

Different paradigms have been used to describe the exam essay, but the most common is IRAC (Issue Rule Application Conclusion). The IRAC paradigm is not without its critics. Fischl and Paul (1999), for example, write '[i]n our combined quarter-century of law teaching – and in the thousands of bluebooks we've read over all those years – neither of us can ever recall seeing an exam answer organized around the so-called IRAC method ("issue-rule-application-conclusion") that was truly first-rate. Not a one.' (1999: 147). Genre-based writing pedagogy, however, foregrounds preparing students to make agentive decisions when engaged in genre practices, rather than produce reductive writing based on formal rules, as objectors to the IRAC paradigm seem to argue. For students writing in a new legal languaculture, teaching paradigms such as IRAC helps to orient them to produce exam answers that professors recognize as genre appropriate. If Strong and Desnoyer (2016) are correct in writing, 'most students' difficulty in law school is not mastering the substantive material, it is demonstrating their knowledge to their professors in a way that the professors recognize and reward,' it is incumbent upon those teaching LLM students to provide instruction that helps students to organize their analysis. Thus, while recognizing criticisms levied at the IRAC paradigm, Kurtz chose to teach IRAC essays to socialize students to genre practices of US legal education. The sections and purpose of the IRAC essay are summarized in Table 3.1.

In an IRAC essay, the Rule and Application sections are tightly linked and where the bulk of a student's grade is earned. In a traditional closed-book exam, the universe of potential law is established by the assigned readings in the course. A well-written essay will cite statutes and cases studied in the course as legal authority. In the rule section, writers are expected to set out each element that must be proven or established on a legal issue. For example, one of the essay prompts in this study required students to analyze a legal question on *self-defense*. There are six elements to self-defense, so in that essay, students would be expected to provide a rule, including any sub-rules and exceptions, for each element.

The application section then walks the reader through each element and sub-rule, analyzing the given facts in light of the legal rules. In a well-written essay, each rule and legal authority cited in the rule section is addressed in the application section. Strong and Desnoyer (2016: 87) recommend, 'do not introduce a case or statute unless it relates to a fact you intend to discuss in the "A" section'. The application section is also not a place to introduce new legal authority; to be applied in the A section, the legal authority must be introduced in the R section, preparing the reader for its relevance. In this way, intratextual references build cohesion in an IRAC essay. Table 3.2 shares an

Table 3.1 IRAC sections and purpose of each section

Section	Purpose
Issue	Identify the legal question(s) implicated by the hypothetical fact pattern. Typically phrased as a question or a *whether*-clause.
Rule	State the legal rule(s) and principle(s) that govern the legal question. Each rule or sub-rule used in the application section must be stated in the rule section. Generally written from broad to narrow.
Application	Analyze what the stated rules mean for the outcome of the given fact pattern. Usually includes the best arguments for 'both sides' and why one is the better argument.
Conclusion	State the most likely outcome of the legal question.

Table 3.2 Example legal analogical reasoning

Legal Analogical Reasoning Example	Elements of Legal Analogical Reasoning
UNLIKE *the tools in Jackson – the sawed-off shotgun, extra shells, masks, and fake license plate* – the items found on Danny Defendant when he was arrested should not be sufficient to show a **substantial step** toward committing robbery. The ski mask and the hastily written note found on Danny Defendant are SIGNIFICANTLY DIFFERENT from the tools in *Jackson* because Danny's items are not indicative of a **clearly formed criminal plot** and thus should not be sufficient to show a **"substantial step"** after the *Jackson* interpretation of what constitutes an attempt.	Demonstrate that the legal concept or category is the impetus for making the analogy. *Make reference to a relevant precedent case fact.* Compare the precedent case fact to an instant case fact. CONVEY THE RELATIONSHIP BETWEEN PRECEDENT AND INSTANT CASE FACTS THROUGH SIGNAL LANGUAGE.

example of what legal analogical reasoning might look like in an IRAC essay. This example was used in the study in a lesson on the language of analogical reasoning. In this example, 'substantial step' would have been identified and defined in the rule as an element of the inchoate crime of attempt.

The example legal analogical reasoning then takes up the legal category (*substantial step*) and conveys how the precedent case differs from the hypo. Here, that entails explaining how items such as a sawed-off shotgun and a fake license plate represent 'clearly formed criminal plot' in a way that a ski mask and a hastily written note do not.

Study Context

The Companion Course

The study was implemented in a legal analysis and law school skills course in the first semester of a one-year pre-LLM program at Mid-Atlantic Law School. The course was co-taught by a Legal Writing Instructor and Kurtz. To socialize students into law school's languacultural norms, the Companion Course used content from the Criminal Law course in which the students were enrolled. Focal cases were selected to provoke development of the students' ability to read and accurately discuss cases, and convey common law legal reasoning. Kurtz developed the Concept-Based Genre Writing pedagogy implemented in the Companion Course. Additionally, Kurtz read all assigned material, attended all class sessions, and took notes in the Criminal Law course. Doing so allowed her access to the discussions of a first-year law classroom and enabled her to transfer any relevant discussions, vocabulary items, or hypotheticals from the Criminal Law Course into the Companion Course for further explication.

Participants

Six students enrolled in the Companion Course, and each agreed to participate in the study. Three students were from Saudi Arabia, two from China, and one from Thailand. Consequently, three students were educated in Islamic law system, and three were prepared in the civil law tradition. Table 3.3 outlines participants' demographic information, including assigned pseudonyms, home country, first language, home legal system, and experience practicing law in their home country.

The Curriculum

Case reading cycles

The judicial opinion serves as the primary teaching tool of US legal education and also, as a genre, is a rich point for international LLM students. To support students in accessing the legal languaculture embodied in the judicial opinion, the Companion Course organized teaching units around Focal Cases discussed in Criminal Law. These units used distributed cognition (see e.g. Brown & Campione, 1996) to disburse responsibility for different aspects of case reading based on identities through which LLM students read a case – Language Learner, Law Student, Legal Problem Solver.

Students were divided into semester-long groups and for each unit, one group was assigned the role of Language Learner, Law Student, Legal Problem Solver. Each reading role group read the focal case for that unit (e.g. for Unit 2, *Commonwealth v. Malone*) and presented analysis based on their assigned reading role. Thus, for each unit, students gained understanding of the focal case from each role – Language Learner (week 1), Law Student (week 2), Legal Problem Solver (week 3) – but were only responsible for a single role for each unit. During the third week of the unit, students wrote an IRAC essay in response to a hypothetical problem. On the day students wrote the IRAC essay in the Companion Course, the focal case was assigned reading for Criminal Law. During the fourth week of each unit, students met with Kurtz individually to discuss their essay, described below in the Languaging phase of C-BLI.

Table 3.3 Demographic information of student-participants

Name	Home country (L1)	Home legal system	Legal practice experience
Fazi	Saudi Arabia (Arabic)	Islamic	Yes, 3 years
Hoobi	Saudi Arabia (Arabic)	Islamic	No
Jun	China (Chinese)	Civil	Yes, 1 year
Omar	Saudi Arabia (Arabic)	Islamic	Yes, 5 months
Pim	Thailand (Thai)	Civil	Yes, 7 years
Yue	China (Chinese)	Civil	No, internships only

Table 3.4 Reading role units

RR unit	Case name	Reading role activity	Legal concept
Teaching Focal Case	*State v. Sophophone*[1]	Analyze as home system lawyers Legal Writing example analysis as common law reasoner	Felony murder
Focal Case 1	*Commonwealth v. Koczwara*, 155 A.2d 825 (Pa. 1959)	Case 1 Language Learner	Strict liability
		Case 1 Law Student	
		Case 1 Legal Problem Solver Case 1 IRAC	
Focal Case 2	*Commonwealth v. Malone*, 47 A.2d 445 (Pa. 1946)	Case 1 IRAC Mediation Sessions Case 2 Language Learner	Depraved heart murder
		Case 2 Law Student	
		Case 2 Legal Problem Solver Case 2 IRAC	
Focal Case 3	*United States v. Jackson*, 180 F.3d 55 (2d. Cir. 1999)	IRAC 2 Mediation Sessions Case 3 Language Learner	
		Case 3 Law Student	
		Case 3 Legal Problem Solver Crim Law Practice Exam	
Focal Case 4	*State v. Norman*, 378 S.E.2d 8 (N.C. 1989)	Practice Exam Mediation Session Case 4 Language Learner	Self-defense (imminent danger)
		Case 4 Law Student	
		Case 4 Legal Problem Solver IRAC 4	
		IRAC 4 Mediation	

[1] The redacted versions of all cases referred to in Chapter 3 and Chapter 4 can be found in Saltzburg *et al.* (2009).

The Concept-Based Genre Writing Curriculum

Concept-based language instruction must confront the 'prior knowledge that students bring to the current instructional situation' (Lantolf & Poehner, 2014: 68), typically referred to as pre-understanding (Miller, 2011). While often this phase is framed as bringing to the fore – making visible – students' spontaneous concepts, when teaching international LLM students, an important part of this phase is making visible students' already internalized scientific concepts. As discussed above, LLM students enter the L2 legal classroom with an already internalized legal languaculture. Thus, the Companion Course instructors intentionally discussed with students how they orient to legal analysis and writing, to make that prior orientation visible to them and available for use as a conceptual tool.

As such, the Companion Course spent several class periods establishing students' pre-understanding of legal analysis. During week 1, Kurtz introduced SCOBAs representing the home legal systems. Students in the course hailed from countries with a primarily civil law (Figure 3.1, below) or Islamic law system. Following the presentation of the SCOBAs, students educated in that legal system were asked to discuss with the class their understanding of the SCOBA and its representation of their home legal system. Students not educated in that legal system could also ask questions about the other legal system.

Following discussion of the home-legal-system SCOBAs, students received instruction in reading hypothetical problems (hypos) and were given the teaching hypo to analyze. Hypos are a common pedagogical tool in US legal education. They present a short factual scenario, a hypothetical situation, intended to trigger a specific legal issue. Students must then apply the appropriate legal rule. In form, hypos can be as short as a professor in class changing one fact of the case being discussed, or as extended as a several-page fact pattern written as a law exam question. Students were asked to read the teaching hypo and analyze it as they would in their home legal system, an activity intended to make their previously internalized legal languaculture available for conscious reflection. The activity served the dual purpose of introducing the students to the hypothetical problem as a common pedagogical tool in US legal education.

Civil Law SCOBA

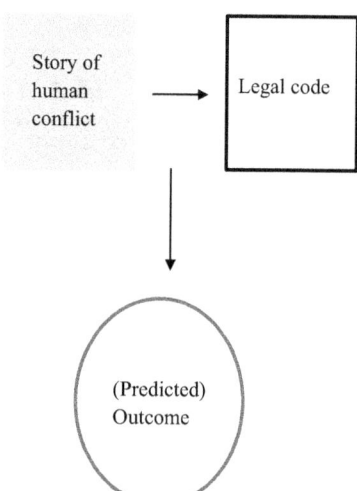

Figure 3.1 Civil law SCOBA

Because the initial iteration of the phases was so intertwined in this study, the Presentation and Materialization phases will be discussed together. In all, four SCOBAs were developed and presented in the Companion Course. Two were presented during the pre-understanding phase, as described above – the SCOBAs representing students' home legal systems. In the presentation phase, a common law SCOBA (Figure 3.2) and legal analogical reasoning SCOBA were presented to students. Development of the legal system SCOBAs attempted to account for both similarities and differences between the legal systems. Therefore, the SCOBA representing each legal system contains several common elements: 'story of human conflict,' 'legal code,' and '(predicted) outcome' categories. 'Story of human conflict' refers to the narrative or real-world conflict that precipitates legal action. In US legal education, this element is typically referred to as 'the facts'.

Given the story of human conflict, legal reasoners must consult the legal texts in their system that control that type of dispute. For example, in a dispute involving a violent assault, a US legal reasoner consults a statute defining levels of assault and case law applying the definitions of these levels to specific sets of facts. As the sources of law differ in the legal systems represented by students in the Companion Course, so too, are different sources of law represented in the SCOBAs. In the same class session that she presented the common law SCOBA, Kurtz also introduced case reading and guided students in collaborative reading of the

Common Law SCOBA

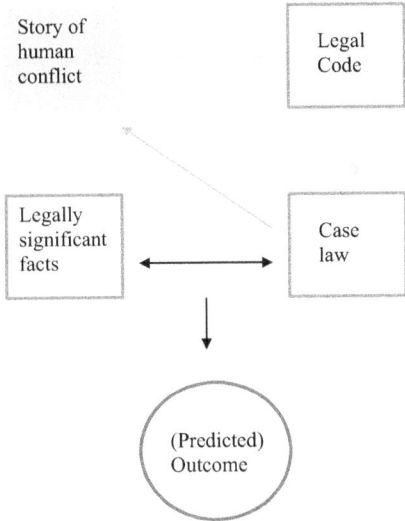

Figure 3.2 Common law SCOBA

34 Concept-Based Language Instruction and Genre-Based Second Language

teaching focal case. In the next class, Legal Writing Instructor modeled common law analysis for the students by mapping her analysis of the teaching hypo onto the common law SCOBA using teaching focal case as precedent.

Legal analogical reasoning was the focal concept of the study because it is a distinguishing feature between legal systems. Thus, legal analogical reasoning (Figure 3.3) was the fourth SCOBA developed for the C-BLI. The legal analogical reasoning SCOBA demonstrates conceptual mappings from source to target domain cases through a series of picture problems. In the SCOBA, 'stories of human conflict' comprised of five different clip art pictures represent a 'client problem' or hypothetical problem. For example, the first picture problem includes clip art of a plumber holding tools in both hands, a hard hat, a wrench, a toolbox, and a water spigot. From this collection of pictures, the legal significance of any one fact is not readily apparent, just as for the novice approaching a hypothetical problem in the common law, which facts are legally relevant is not clarified until one has consulted precedent cases. The analogical reasoning SCOBA is replicated in Figure 3.3 with text boxes standing in for the clip art pictures.

In the SCOBA, precedent cases are represented by two pictures on the right-hand side. Three such precedent cases are present in Figure 3.3 – a firefighter and water valve on a pipe, a briefcase and a man at a computer, and a paint tray with a painting roller and three cans of paint. The SCOBA was designed so that the 'legal category' in the precedent case must be explicitly stated before a student returns to the client case to select analogous facts. For example, one possible legal category created by Precedent Case 1 is 'Used as a protective barrier.' Refracted through this category, the significant client case facts become the plumber and the hard hat. A different category would render different facts salient.

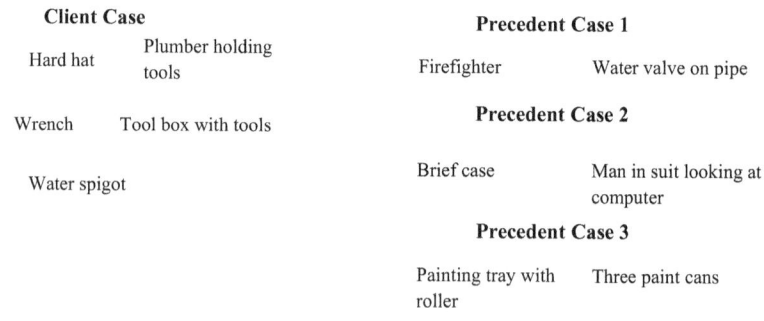

Analogical Reasoning SCOBA

Figure 3.3 Analogical reasoning SCOBA

Approaching analogical reasoning in this way reinforces that legal analogical reasoning is constrained by the legal categories established by statutes and prior case law. Because students were forced to abstract relationships (legal categories) from stories of conflict (here, pictures), the process of making connections not immediately apparent in our conceptual systems was simulated, thereby reconstituting how specific facts were viewed (Winter, 2001). As the course transitioned to problem-solving activity using the common law and legal analogical reasoning SCOBAs, the necessity of connecting the legal concept and the factual comparisons being made was a point that required continued social mediation.

So that students had continual access to the materializations, each received printed copies of the SCOBAs to use as they analyzed legal problems. The common law SCOBA was also printed on a large poster board to be written on during class analysis of legal problems. Additionally, at times, specific portions of the SCOBA were also replicated in PowerPoint slides or on the classroom whiteboard to focus class analysis of a legal problem.

The languaging phase of the C-BLI study was carried out in individual meetings with students to discuss their IRAC essays. In each of four sessions, Kurtz discussed with students their understanding of the focal case, common law analysis, and decisions they made writing each IRAC essay. Kurtz grounded her mediation in these individual meetings in *interactionist dynamic assessment* (e.g. Lantolf & Poehner, 2004). Dynamic assessment is an approach to understanding developed and developing learner capabilities that 'functions as both an assessment and an instructional session as these become a seamless activity concerned with understanding learners' abilities by promoting their development' (Poehner, 2008a: 34). In interactionist dynamic assessment, mediation is negotiated with the individual or group of learners and 'continually adjusted in accordance with the learner's responsivity' (Feuerstein *et al.*, 1979: 102). Due to the focus on responsivity from the learner, interactionist dynamic assessment provides a teacher-researcher with rich information about how to attune mediation to promote student development. Languaging with students from an interactionist dynamic assessment perspective involves a 'handing over' of responsibility for regulation of the shared performance. Initially, the teacher takes primary responsibility, but gradually passes increased responsibility to the learner (Karpov & Gindis, 2000) as the learner develops control over her performance of the concepts taught.

In the performance phase, students use the academic concept in practical, goal-oriented activity. Here, that entailed using analogical reasoning in legal problem solving through both speaking and writing. Kurtz and Legal Writing Instructor engaged the students in class discussion of hypothetical legal problems whereby students needed to use the focal precedent cases in their analysis. Additionally, students wrote six IRAC essays throughout the semester, where they were required to use analogical reasoning in their analysis – twice collaboratively with their Reading Role partner, and four times independently in class under exam conditions. For each independently written IRAC essay, students met with Kurtz to discuss their writing. These essays and the mediation sessions form the primary basis for data analysis in the study.

In this course, the C-BLI phases were not stepwise. The languaging and performance phases were repeated through each reading role cycle. The SCOBAs were available and used as mediation throughout the semester as deemed necessary by students or instructors. While the course may not have, for example, returned formally to the presentation phase, the students were continually asked to perform and then provided mediation to support further development in understanding legal analogical reasoning and its role in US legal analysis.

Data sources and analysis

The IRAC essays were analyzed for evidence of development of analogical reasoning in two steps. First, a modified obligatory occasion analysis was conducted to determine whether or not analogical reasoning was present in the essay. Any reference to a legal case by name or a recognizable case fact was coded as presence of analogical reasoning. Second, all presence of analogical reasoning was compared to the definition of legal analogical reasoning described above. If an analogy satisfied all four elements of the definition (1) demonstrated that the legal concept or category was the impetus for making the analogy; (2) made reference to a relevant precedent case fact; (3) compared the precedent case fact to an instant case fact; and (4) conveyed the relationship between precedent and instant case facts through 'signal language,' it was coded legal analogical reasoning. If an analogy did not satisfy all four elements, it was coded as developing analogical reasoning. The categories of developing analogical reasoning produced in this study are further described in Kurtz (2017).

All class sessions of the Companion Course, Reading Role meetings, and individual mediation sessions with Kurtz were video recorded and transcribed using Inqscribe. The video recordings and the accompanying transcripts were used to identify and trace microgenetic changes in learner understanding and writing over time.

Analyzing development

Following a V-SCT approach, each data source was analyzed to understand the extent to which changed understanding of legal analogical reasoning was evident. That is, the data was analyzed for evidence of student development or internalization of the focal concept of the study.

Vygotsky's theory of development describes a 'process characterized by periodicity, unevenness in the development of different functions, metamorphosis or qualitative transformations of one form into another, intertwining of external and internal factors,' also referring to this unevenness of development as 'upheavals' (1978: 73). As discussed in Chapter 2, internalization is the ability to use a concept in practical, goal-oriented activity relatively quickly without reliance on external tools (e.g. teaching aids or social mediation). Along the way students may display 'upheavals' in their understanding of the concept under study; in their orientation to practical, goal-oriented activity; and in their use of tools available to them that assist their use of the concept in goal-oriented activity. These shifts and changes are what teacher-researchers in a C-BLI program attune to as they relate to the revolutionary and non-linear nature of academic development. In this study, particular analytic focus was paid to verbalizations and writing where a student's understanding of legal analogical reasoning appeared to be shifting and thus ripe for mediation.

Students' engagement with and use of legal analogical reasoning was analyzed for presence of such moments of upheaval. 'Upheavals' took the form of change in the presence or absence of analogical reasoning in student written legal analysis, change in the quality of analogies in written legal analysis, quality of the engagement with social mediation offered by the instructors and the C-BLI. The genesis of these upheavals, how the student engaged the social and/or conceptual mediation, and any ultimate change in legal analogical reasoning performance or understanding received analytical focus; wherever possible, interpretation of upheavals and development is triangulated through multiple data sources, such as multiple interactions in close succession or through a written artifact and an oral interaction.

4 Legal Writing: Findings and Implications

Legal Analogical Reasoning

One must develop the ability to reason by analogy to gain full access to the legal discourse community in a US law school. To highlight the way discipline-specific analogical reasoning is used in legal discourse, the term *legal analogical reasoning* is adopted. *Legal analogies* (1) are refracted through legal categories which are the impetus for making the analogy; (2) make reference to a relevant precedent case fact/reasoning; (3) compare the precedent case fact to an instant case fact; and (4) convey the relationship between precedent and instant case facts through 'signal language.' Here, signal language refers to sentence structure and word choice that explicitly mark the relationship between the precedent case and the case under analysis. In an IRAC essay such analogical reasoning also tends to be conceptually and linguistically condensed. That is, rather than other legal genres, such as the judicial opinion or office memorandum, where sometimes extensive background is provided for precedent cases, in an IRAC essay, analogical reasoning tends to occur at the sentential level, often with a first mention in the rule and the analogy appearing in the application.

Further, a hallmark of developing as a legal reasoner is the ability to 'argue both sides,' that is, the ability to make each party's best argument, in addition to a normative prediction as to which argument is more likely to prevail. Law classes spend considerable time and effort leading students to 'see both sides' of a legal situation and develop the ability to present an argument for the outcome desired by either party. In this study, analogies that demonstrated such ability were coded *ironic legal analogies*, as this term highlights the underlying cognitive ability. Following Egan's (1998) discussion of *ironic understanding* as the most developed form of human thinking, ironic analogies refer to a legal thinker's ability to transcend her own perspective in analyzing a legal problem. Irony here refers to a way of thinking, which Egan argues transcends even scientific thinking. As Egan notes, '[t]he fluent ironist can slip from perspective to perspective' (Egan, 1998: 145). A hallmark of good legal reasoning is the ability to anticipate the opposing party's perspective, their argument, in order to pre-emptively rebut it. As such, an important goal of LLM instruction is to promote students' ability to use the same case to produce legal analogies for both sides of an argument.

Developmental trajectories in legal analogical reasoning are presented in Table 4.1. By the end of the semester, three students (Hoobi, Jun, and Yue) produced legal analogies in their writing, while three (Fazi, Omar, Pim) were still developing control over legal analogical reasoning in their written legal analysis. At least three developmental trajectories related to analogical reasoning emerged. Further discussion of these developmental trajectories, including a case study of one student exhibiting each trajectory is presented in Kurtz (2017). The first developmental trajectory, exhibited by Hoobi and Yue, is one where analogical reasoning is attempted in each writing until legal analogical reasoning emerges.

The second developmental trajectory revealed is that of Omar, who did not use analogical reasoning in any IRAC essay. The third developmental path, revealed in Table 4.1, is one of uneven use of analogical reasoning. Fazi, Jun, and Pim each used analogical reasoning in several IRAC essays but did not in at least one essay. Of the students who exhibit this developmental path, only Jun produced legal analogies in any IRAC essay. Although he attempted analogical reasoning in the first IRAC essay, he did not use it in the second essay. In IRAC essay 3, Jun again employed analogical reasoning, and in the fourth IRAC essay, Jun produced legal analogies. From a V-SCT perspective, uneven progression is often indicative of development. In Jun's case, what at times appears to be regression is actually indicative of destabilization of his preconceived notions of legal discourse so that new understanding of legal discourse can emerge.

In the semester reported on here, no student used ironic analogical reasoning in their writing, but Hoobi, Yue, and Jun each did in collaborative activity. That is, no IRAC essay analyzed the strongest argument for both parties in the hypo's dispute. However, Yue produced

Table 4.1 Legal analogical reasoning developmental trajectories

Student	IRAC 1	IRAC 2	IRAC 3	IRAC 4
Fazi	−	+	−	+
Hoobi	+	+	++	++
Jun	+	−	+	++
Omar	−	−	−	−
Pim	+	−	+	−
Yue	+	+	+	++

Note: − = no analogical reasoning; + = incomplete analogical reasoning; ++ = legal analogical reasoning ironic analogies in class (week 10) and in her IRAC 4 mediation session. Hoobi demonstrated the ability to make the argument for both sides in class (week 9) and through a chart in IRAC essay 4. The analysis was not considered genre-appropriate writing because it was presented in a grammatically reduced chart rather than in prose. Similarly, Jun also demonstrated the burgeoning ability to produce ironic analogies in collaboration with conceptual mediation (the common law SCOBA) and in social mediation from Kurtz.

Jun

Jun held a bachelor's degree in law (LLB) from a Chinese university. He practiced corporate law in Shanghai, China, for one year before enrolling in the pre-LLM program. Jun indicated on his pre-semester questionnaire that his home country uses a civil law system, but officially the People's Republic of China characterizes its legal system as a Socialist Legal System with Uniquely Chinese Characteristics (Chow, 2023). He was pursuing the LLM because: *I think law is very interesting. in the future I want to be a lawyer. I love American law. It also can improve much precious experiences (pre-semester questionnaire)*. As such, Jun's stated purpose for pursuing the LLM degree indicated an interest in US law, but also personal and social reasons for the experience.

Jun was frequently quiet in class, rarely volunteering answers, but when called on, offered thoughtful contributions that pushed the classroom conversation forward. Jun also seemed capable of and enjoyed assisting other students with language issues such as specific vocabulary questions. When other students expressed confusion about a specific word, Jun was frequently the first student to offer a succinct and correct answer. For example, when his semester-long reading partner asked what *shout* meant during a small group meeting with Kurtz, Jun supplied, *a loud talking* (Week 13) before Kurtz responded.

When Jun volunteered contributions to class, he posed questions indicating active engagement and a deep understanding of the material. In fact, his questions sometimes demonstrated quite sophisticated uptake of US legal education's teaching tools. For example, during another group's Legal Problem Solver presentation in Week 10, Jun asked, '*what if someone did not participate in the planning but got in the car right before the drive to the burglary?*' This question demonstrates sophisticated engagement with the legal concept (attempt) and followed a question pattern common in US legal education as his question altered one hypo fact in a potentially legally significant way. Jun's question anticipates the sort of hypo a professor might propose and implicates legal analogical reasoning. Essentially, Jun asks a question about how the precedent case might be applied differently, through legal analogical reasoning, to this novel (and relevant) factual scenario.

Analysis of Jun's development as a common law legal writer

The following analysis traces Jun's development as a common law reasoner throughout the semester of the study. Particular emphasis is placed on interactions with Kurtz and submitted IRAC essays that demonstrate 'disruptions' in Jun's understanding of legal analogical reasoning. That is, following V-SCT, the analysis adopts a genetic approach in understanding legal analogical reasoning through Jun's unfolding development in legal analogical reasoning, paying analytic attention to mediation received and changes in the ability over time.

Students hand-wrote their IRAC essays in class. In this chapter, Jun's analysis has been typed for ease of reading, but it is presented typographically as close to his handwritten analysis as possible to include agentive, online decisions he made as a writer. For example, if Jun originally wrote a word and then crossed it out, this is represented by typing what was crossed out with the strikethrough, as presented in his essay (e.g. in Excerpt 4.1 Jun corrected spelling: ~~lisense~~ license). For readability, transcripts are verbatim, with only pauses indicated through (.), or the number of seconds of a pause, as in a three-second pause represented by (3).

Concept development in legal analogical reasoning

In his first IRAC essay (Excerpt 4.1), Jun used analogical reasoning, but this attempt demonstrated nascent ability to employ *legal* analogical reasoning. Two nodes for analysis are relevant in this excerpt. First, Jun has produced a case-concept mismatch, a theme which will carry throughout his writing in the first semester. Second, Jun has produced an analogy in which the precedent case and hypo remain distinct entities.

Excerpt 4.1. Case-concept mismatch and conceptually distinct treatment of cases

> Compare with the koczwara case, koczwara has ~~lisense~~ license selling alcohol drinks, his employee sold alcohol drinks to minors who are not accompanied ~~by~~ with their parents ore any supervisor. His employee also allowed the minors to frequent the tavern two times who are not accompanied by their parents ~~and~~ or supervisors. The justice finally ~~think~~ decided to ~~find~~ fine koczwara 500$ since he violate the federal liquor act.
>
> In instant case, Tommy is only a employee of Joey's Gas Station, he has ~~on~~ no license to sell the cigarettes. Although ~~he~~ Timmy is owner of a truck and he is responsible for delivering cigarettes to Gas Station, these actions didn't have to acquire a license. Tommy's whole action was arranged by his employer, the owner of the Gas Station.

A case-concept mismatch occurs when a writer uses a precedent case to analyze a legal concept other than the legal concept actually at issue or refracts the case through a legal concept the case does not actually embody. In the Criminal Law casebook, Focal Case 1 embodied two legal concepts – strict liability and vicarious liability – but the bulk of class discussion foregrounded strict liability, and the hypo was written to invoke strict liability rather than vicarious liability.

Jun's rule section referred to strict liability, but his application appears to analyze vicarious liability, an intratextual mismatch. His inclusion of the employee–employer relationship in Focal Case 1 and creation of facts not in the hypo about an employee–employer relationship are indicative of this analysis. Thus, from a legal analogical reasoning perspective, Jun's analogical reasoning in IRAC essay 1 is not yet appropriate because he has selected the inappropriate legal concept – a case-concept mismatch. Although the source of the mismatch is arguably reading, the case-concept mismatch implicates written legal analogies because appropriate connection of facts to both precedent case and hypo is a prerequisite for legal analogical reasoning. This mismatch is also an area for writing development because in an IRAC, the application section should analyze all legal principles presented in the rule section.

Jun's analysis in Excerpt 4.1 also demonstrates he has not yet developed control over how to conceptually map the reasoning of the precedent case to the case under analysis. He writes one entire paragraph recounting the facts of Focal Case 1 and follows that with a paragraph about the facts of the hypo. Although he uses appropriate signal language to begin each paragraph *Compare with the koczwara case* and *In instant case* – in this first IRAC, conceptually and syntactically the precedent and hypo remain discrete entities, and there is not yet connection of the facts or reasoning present. In essence, the facts of the precedent case and hypo are written consecutively, without conceptual mapping of what the one (Focal Case 1) means for the other (hypo).

Despite attempting analogical reasoning in his first IRAC essay, in the second, Jun did not refer to case law at all. While he may have appropriated some of the terminology (e.g. provocation) from case law, Jun relied on rule-based reasoning in IRAC 2. His application section restated facts of the hypo and at the end of each paragraph drew a legal conclusion (e.g. *A reasonable person in this situation must be cool down*; *In this situation I think a reasonable person cannot provoke himself*). Since Jun had previously attempted analogical reasoning, Kurtz opened the mediation session by asking him why he did not use it in this essay.

After 14 seconds of thinking time, Jun responds that he '*want to try the difference* because for the previous IRAC essay he *made the comparison but in this case I didn't make some comparison.*' Kurtz responded to Jun's acknowledgement that he used analogical reasoning in IRAC 1 but not this IRAC by asking why he chose not to use analogical reasoning in this essay. Jun's response indicated two reasons – one a lexical recall issue and one a conceptual legal analogical reasoning issue.

Initially, Kurtz addressed the '*don't know the case name exactly*' issue and advised Jun in lines deleted here that in exam writing when he cannot remember a specific case name, he can refer to the most

Excerpt 4.2 'I want to try the difference'

```
1   K   did you try to write this essay differently from how
2           you wrote that one
3   J   (1) mm (14) i uh i want to try the difference but uh
4           because uh in previous case i made the i made the
5           comparison but uh in this case i didn't make some
6           comparison
7   K   yeah so why did you choose not to make the
8           comparisons in this case
9   J   uh (2) because i think uh it's different from the
10          previous each previous case and i actually want to
11          comparison but i don't know the case name exactly
```

salient fact of the case – e.g. referring to Focal Case 2, *Commonwealth v. Malone*, as '*the Russian poker case.*' In a pedagogic genre such as the IRAC essay, this strategy allows students who cannot recall a specific case name to engage in the rhetorical expectations of the genre – to state rules from cases studied in class and to reason with those cases. In the exam context, the universe of potential law is limited; the professor has assigned the only potential cases that can be used as legal authority. For example, in the Criminal Law course, only one assigned case involved so-called Russian poker. Thus, if a student could not recall the name *Commonwealth v. Malone*, a professor, the only reader of a law school exam, would understand which case a student meant with a phrase such as '*the Russian poker case.*' Addressing case name recall, then, was useful for Jun as he subsequently took up this strategy to externalize analysis even when he could not recall a case name (see e.g. Excerpt 4.6).

When Kurtz and Jun returned to the conceptual issue of legal analogical reasoning in the IRAC 2 mediation session, Jun offered first-degree murder as a potential outcome for the defendant in the hypo, citing premeditation as a legal concept critical to analyzing the legal problem. Jun further identified *Commonwealth v. Carroll*, 194 A.2d 911 (Pa. 1963) as the first-degree murder case he wanted to apply to the hypo. Excerpt 4.3 occurs just after Kurtz and Jun established that this was a case where a man shot his wife in the head while she slept and that the court in that case reasoned that premeditation could be developed in the time it took the defendant to grab the gun from the windowsill and pull the trigger.

In lines 1–12, Kurtz modeled the analogical reasoning process for Jun. She connected each of the requisite components of analogical

Excerpt 4.3 'Each case they rose from an argument'

1	K	so we decided we learned from Carroll that
2		premeditation can be developed this intent can be
3		developed in a short amount of time and the man who
4		killed his wife by grabbing the gun from the
5		windowsill that was enough to satisfy this intent
6		this willful deliberate premeditated killing and you
7		decided the facts you're going to use for the hypo
8		is he was hiding behind the pillar waiting for the
9		victim there'd been this previous argument um do
10		these facts are they as are they equally as strong
11		as carroll are they stronger than carroll are they
12		weaker than carroll for premeditation
13	J	uh (5) because us this boxer boxer is u h he is a
14		former professional heavyweight boxer he know he is
15		very powerful so ah i think he hu himself is ah have
16		enough capability to make a dangerous make dangerous
17		so if if he want to intend to kill him just a though
18		it finish the premeditation and hide the hide the
19		pillar
20	K	okay so what does his what does his having his being
21		a former boxer what does that have to do with
22		premeditation
23	J	(.) mm (6) he's premeditation mm
24	K	cuz these facts were the facts you told me were
25		important for the premeditation here so i just wanna
26		know if this case said yes premeditation because we
27		can look at these circumstances and infer
28		premeditation what do these what comparison can we

29		make between these two cases to determine whether or
30		not a court would say there's premeditation here
31	J	ah yes in this case uh the defendant didn't prepare
32		long times to make a premeditation it's a very short
33		times and in this case it's same too
34	K	mm hmm
35	J	yes
36	K	so they're similar in that there's not a long time
37		there's not a long time span right when um to show
38		this premeditation
39	J	yes
40	K	do you have any facts that you can argue are
41		stronger than Carroll for this premeditation
42	J	mm (14) because the each case uh uh they rose from
43		an argument and each case uh the defendant is very
44		angry and each case they have a short preparation
45		it's very same with the premeditation

reasoning – the legal concept (premeditation in first-degree murder); a case representative of the legal concept (*Commonwealth v. Carroll*); factual information from the case with which to develop analogies ('*that this man who killed his wife by picking up the gun from the windowsill and shooting*'); and this understanding leads one to the precipice of legal analogical reasoning ('*you decided the facts you're going to use for the hypo is he was hiding behind the pillar waiting for the victim [and] there'd been this previous argument*'). Kurtz then hands responsibility over to Jun when she asks him to complete the conceptual mapping.

Jun responds by focusing again on the defendant's status as a former heavyweight boxer, the same facts he had used in his original analysis. Kurtz questions the focus on these facts, because they represent facts useful for analysis of a different level of homicide. She asks Jun what the connection is between the defendant's status as a former heavyweight boxer and premeditation. Jun thinks for six seconds, says, '*he's premeditation*' and stops. Kurtz redirects Jun's attention ('*because these were the facts you told me were important for premeditation*') and again models the conceptual mapping of legal analogical reasoning.

This mediation focuses Jun on an important part of premeditation analysis in *Carroll* – planning time. He indicates that the cases are the same because *'the defendant didn't prepare long times to make a premeditation it's a very short times and in this case it's same too.'* In this excerpt, collaboratively, Kurtz and Jun have completed legal analogical reasoning. In lines 1–12 and 24–30 Kurtz explicitly models the legal analogical reasoning process, with Jun completing the analogy in lines 42–45. With social mediation, then, Jun completes legal analogical reasoning for the first observable time. For Jun, like other students in this study, legal analogies emerge in collaboration with Kurtz before they emerge in autonomous written legal analysis.

Three weeks later, Jun demonstrated further development in IRAC 3. In that essay, Excerpt 4.4, Jun exhibited emerging control over case-concept connections, conceptually blending cases in legal analogical reasoning.

Excerpt 4.4. 'the dirty needle, like one bullet gun and dangerous dog'

~Piaget exchanged the clean needle to drug addicts, which is a good purpose, she didn't want anyone to be infected with AIDS, instead she want to prevent drug addicts from cross infection. She had no intention to kill anyone. In Malone's case, Malone and victim played Russia game which cause the death of victim. In commonwealth v. Carroll the defendant kill his wife by shot the head twice causing the death of victim, he has intention to kill and he finally be convicted to the first degree murder. A dirty needles, which has high possibility to cause someone to be infected with disease, was mixed in the clean needles by defendant. she must know this fact and just let everything continue. In Commonwealth v. Malone defendant highly knew that the gun could cause the death of person, and he still do that. In People v. Knoller, the dog owner who realized that her dog has great threat to other and she just unlock her dog swing outside the room. In this case, Piaget notice that the dirty needle is very dangerous, she just handed out another person who need a clean one, and the victim finally death from the disease which caused by the dirty needle.
~the dirty needle, like one bullet gun and dangerous dog, each of them are highly possible to take people's life. Piaget, in her mind didn't want anyone die, but her gross recklessness cause the victim's death.

Here, Jun demonstrates developing control over connecting the language of legal concepts with relevant legal cases – moving toward discourse-appropriate case-concept match. That entailed accurately matching the language of different *mens rea* levels with cases exemplifying that category of homicide. *Mens rea* language for each case is significant not only because this language distinguishes the depraved heart murder cases (a category of second-degree murder) from the first-degree murder case, but also because Jun accurately incorporated these distinctions into his analysis. For example, Jun appropriately connects first-degree murder with *'intention to kill'* and connects this language with the first-degree murder case *Carroll*. In referring to each of the other defendants, Jun employed lesser *mens rea* language, signaling a different level of culpability – defendant **highly knew** that the gun **could cause the death** of a person and he still do that (Commonwealth v. Malone); the *dog owner who **realized** that her dog has **great threat** to other and she just unlock her dog swing outside the room (People v. Knoller,* 158 P.3d 731 (Cal. 2007)); (emphases added). Thus, IRAC essay 3 constituted evidence of development from the second IRAC mediation session, where Jun and Kurtz discussed linking precedent cases with the legal categories they invoke.

Additionally, unlike his previous essays, Jun has conceptually condensed his analysis so that precedent cases are more clearly mapped onto the case at hand. Unlike previous writings, Jun integrates into the same paragraph discussion of precedent cases and the hypo. This indicates a move toward conceptual connection between case facts and legal categories, whereas previously each case was presented as a discrete entity in its own paragraph. In the main analytical paragraph in Excerpt 4.4, all case discussion is still presented sentence by sentence, and is not yet linked by signal language identifying the conceptual relation, but organization at the paragraph level is moving toward conceptual integration. That is, Jun is moving toward agentively applying the precedent cases to the hypo.

Although to some extent the legal analogy must be inferred, in IRAC 3, it is possible to make this inference. Jun has appropriately identified *mens rea* language for the first-degree murder case and the two depraved heart murder cases he uses as precedent. The language referring to defendant Piaget's culpability much more closely resembles his language referring to the depraved heart murder cases, *Malone* and *Knoller*, than the first-degree murder case, *Carroll*, signaling that he likely is analyzing the hypo as a depraved heart murder case. Jun's language is target-like in that it reflects an appropriate concept-case mapping, although it does not explicitly signal this relationship or explain how and why running a needle exchange for drug addicts should have the same legal culpability as owning two large dogs one cannot control. Conceptually, though, Jun's analogical reasoning in IRAC 3 indicated awareness of and developing control over the ability to link precedent cases to the legal concepts that they represented and make this connection clear to the reader.

The final sentence of Jun's application section for IRAC 3 demonstrates a movement toward discursive integration necessary for legal analogical reasoning, especially in an IRAC essay. In this sentence, Jun distilled the precedent cases and hypo case to the most dangerous fact in each – the dirty needle (hypo), one bullet gun (*Malone*), and dangerous dog (*Knoller*). Jun signals the dirty needle in the hypo is similar to the dangerous item in each of the precedent cases through the use of *like* and explains that '*each of them are highly possible to take people's life.*' Jun concluded the application section by explicitly invoking a *mens rea* term when he writes *Piaget in her mind didn't want anyone die, but her **gross recklessness** cause the victim's death* (emphasis added). The ability to distill the precedent cases down to the defendant's actions related to the knowledge of the danger in each case and acting anyway suggests a developing understanding of the use of analogical reasoning and precedent in the common-law system. At this point, Jun demonstrates ability to use legal concepts to categorize seemingly disparate items. That is, a used needle, a loaded gun, and a large-breed dog are items not likely to have established connections in the everyday minds of people, but Jun recognizes that in legal analogical reasoning, these items may indeed be legally comparable.

Two weeks later, for his Legal Problem Solver presentation, Jun submitted hypo analysis indicating yet further development. For this Reading Role Cycle, Kurtz instructed Jun and Hoobi, Jun's partner, to present their hypo analysis using an electronic version of the common law SCOBA. They were asked to use a Microsoft Word file of the SCOBA to present their analysis of hypo using the Focal Case for that unit as precedent. Each student was asked to present one 'side' of the analysis; Kurtz assigned Jun analysis that indicated the imminent danger element *did not* exist, and therefore a self-defense argument would not be successful. Hoobi was instructed to present the opposite argument. Jun submitted a two-page Microsoft Word document that contained both arguments; the information in each box for both SCOBAs (Figure 4.1, Figure 4.2) was the same except for the 'Legally Relevant Facts' for the hypo. In that box, Jun included different facts from the same hypo that he relied on for analogical reasoning to reach the two different outcomes – yes or no imminent danger was present or not.

The analysis that Jun submitted indicated even further development from the analysis he produced in IRAC 3. In fact, Jun's fact selection indicated development toward the ability to produce *ironic analogies*. Figures 4.1 and 4.2 demonstrate Jun drawing upon different facts of the hypo to reach both a 'yes' and a 'no' analysis. Apparently, then, conceptual mediation, in the form of the SCOBA, assisted Jun in organizing the relevant aspects of the analysis. This organization allowed Jun to produce facts for analogical reasoning that would lead to *ironic analogies*, the production of which is an ultimate goal of legal education. Although Jun had yet to produce legal analogical reasoning in an IRAC essay, in the Legal Problem Solver presentation, through engagement with the SCOBA, Jun drew on relevant facts that would lead him to produce ironic analogies. Thus, Jun demonstrates the ability to do the *reasoning* to produce legal analogies. To display more complete control over legal analogical reasoning or ironic analogies, however, Jun would need to produce the analogies in written legal analysis, such as in an IRAC essay.

In IRAC 4, Jun produced legal analogical reasoning for the first time in written performance. The Legal Problem Solver presentation and IRAC 4 were written in response to different hypos but were both in the unit focused on *State v. Norman* (1989). One element of Jun's self-defense analysis is reproduced in Excerpt 4.5, but Jun provided similar analysis for three of the six elements of self-defense in his IRAC essay.

Excerpt 4.5. 'Derrick had more imminent danger than Norman'

The most controversial fact is imminent danger. In this case, Derrick defendant saw that Vick decedent had a gun and watched Derrick defendant and his car. In Norman's case, the defendant killed his huband who was sleeping and never poccessed a ~~g~~ some weapon that can threat the ~~defendant~~ Norman defendant in short time. Comparing these two case, Derrick more ~~likely~~ had ∧ more ∧ imminent danger than Norman.

First, Jun has identified imminent danger as the most important element to analyze in this hypo, a feature new to his written legal analysis. This demonstrates that Jun is learning to discriminate between legal controversies and facts actually at issue and those that are not. This paragraph is also more tightly organized around a single legal concept than has been observed in Jun's previous analysis. Each sentence supports

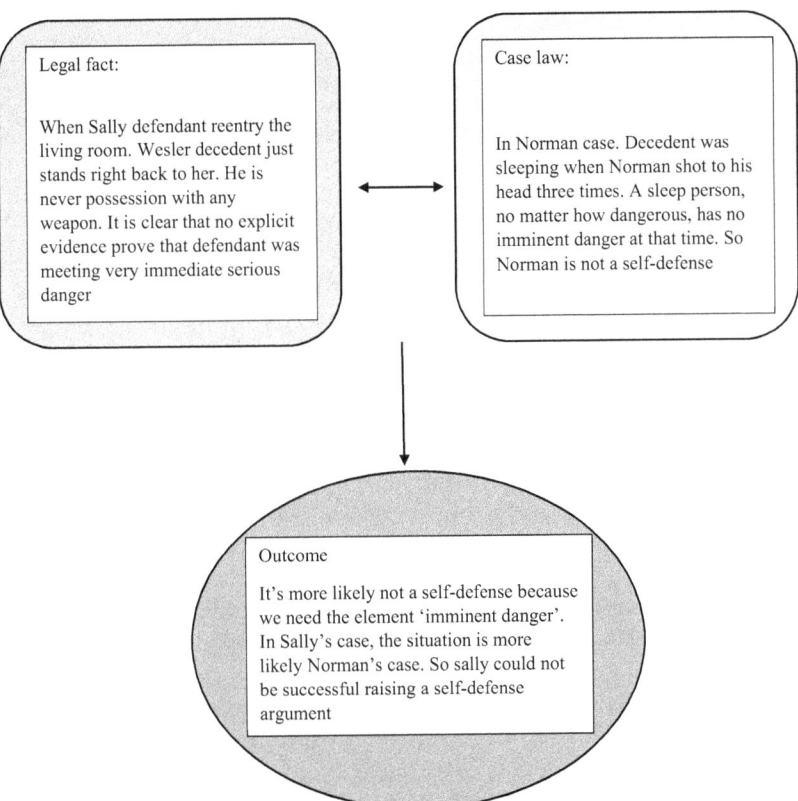

Figure 4.1 Jun's analysis of NO imminent danger

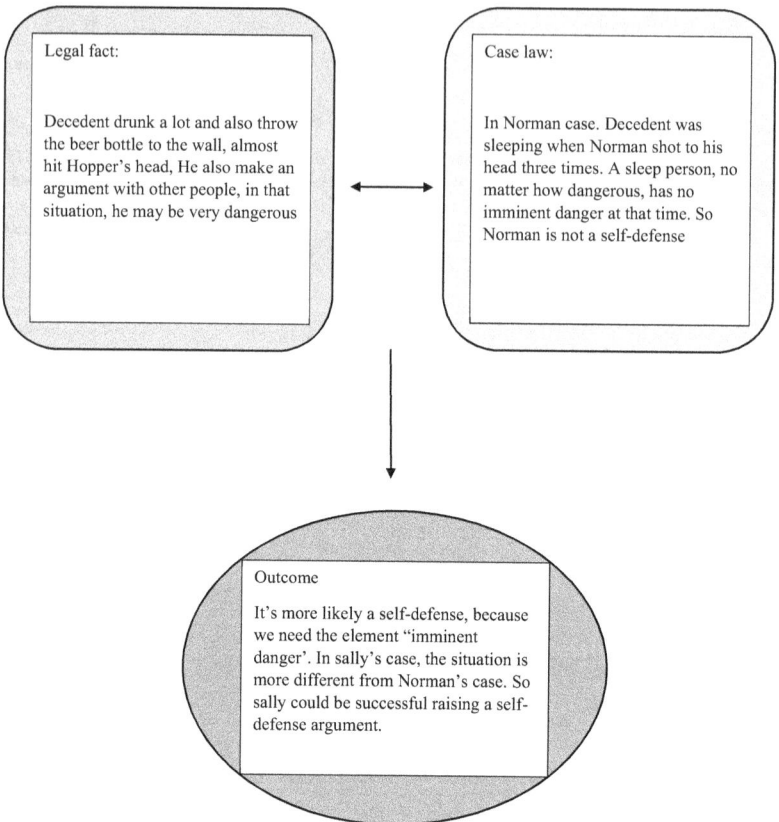

Figure 4.2 Jun's analysis of YES imminent danger

analysis of imminent danger and imminent danger only. In both precedent case fact selection and hypo case fact selection, Jun demonstrates development toward case-concept match.

Jun also appears to be developing in close reading of the hypos, as indicated where Jun originally started to write a word beginning with a *g* (presumably *gun*) but changed his mind and wrote *some weapon*. While *gun* is a more concrete term than *some weapon*, the hypo was written to implicate analysis on this very point. In the hypo, the defendant *thought* the person he shot was holding a gun, but careful reading of the hypo will indicate the decedent was actually holding a cordless drill.

Still, there is room for further development. In comments provided on the IRAC essay prior to Kurtz's mediation session with Jun, Legal Writing Instructor wrote: *Facts missing about imminent danger – what about the fact that the victim was facing away (got shot in the back) at the time of the attack? Or that the fight had happened earlier and the defendant went home and got a gun (like Norman) or that the defendant was in a moving car and the victim was on foot?* Legal Writing Instructor's comments suggest that while conceptually Jun is internalizing the ability to select appropriate facts and use them to make legal arguments, to fully develop as a common law reasoner, he will need to elaborate and extend this ability to include analysis of all legally relevant facts. Indeed, IRAC 4 was Jun's longest of the semester at 435 words. Both his rule and application sections indicate further analytical elaboration is necessary. For reference, Strong and Desnoyer (2016) include six student-produced IRAC essays as examples in their book. The mean length of those essays is 874 words, indicating Jun should produce further analysis to approach genre expectations. Still, Jun's IRAC 4 demonstrates considerable development in legal analogical reasoning, as does his interaction with Kurtz in the mediation session (Excerpt 4.6).

Notably, the instructional conversation in Excerpt 4.6 is quite different from earlier mediation sessions. Initially, Kurtz asks about the element imminent danger and Jun, without the thinking time necessary in earlier sessions, provides the relevant case (*'this case should compare with sleeping husband case'*), connects that case to the concept, and provides the outcome of his analysis (*'it's much less imminent danger than this case ... this case has imminent danger'*). Accepting this utterance as sufficiently mapping conceptual relations from the precedent case onto the hypo, Kurtz probes how Jun thinks the decedent in the hypo is more dangerous than the decedent in Focal Case 4. Again, without thinking time, Jun supplies two facts from the hypo (*'he has conscious and he possessing a gun in his hand'*).

Again, Jun demonstrates further internalized understanding of applying precedent cases in legal analysis when, in Excerpt 4.7 he initially suggests premeditation (first-degree murder) as a potential concept useful in analysis. When Kurtz questions this suggestion, Jun immediately backtracks.

Throughout the semester, a continued focus of Kurtz's mediation was the appropriate connection of case and legal concept necessary for legal analogical reasoning. In Excerpt 4.7 when Jun again provides a potential case-concept mismatch and Kurtz questions that selection, Jun immediately identifies *'no we talk about imminent danger'* and supplies an appropriate fact to use in the analysis of imminent danger, whether or not the victim in the hypo was holding a dangerous weapon (*'if he just holding a cordless drill maybe it's no imminent danger'*). Jun also orally produces an ironic analogy by immediately supplying both a prosecution and a defense argument – the defendant thought he saw a gun (defense argument) but actually the victim was holding a cordless drill (prosecution argument), again a display of development that occurs in social mediation and with access to conceptual mediation before it emerges in written performance.

Excerpt 4.6 'More imminent danger than the sleeping man'

1	K	ahm how about imminent danger
2	J	ah i think uh this case should compare with sleeping
3		husband
4	K	mm hmm
5	J	case because in that case a man was sleeping ah it's
6		it's much less imminent danger than this case
7	K	okay
8	J	and in this case is more imminent danger than the
9		sleeping man so i think compare this case this case
10		has imminent danger
11	K	okay so how is the victim in this case more
12		dangerous than the sleeping man
13	J	because he had conscious and he possessing a gun in
14		his hand

Discussion and Conclusions

Two themes were salient in Jun's development of legal analogical reasoning – the case-concept mismatch and conceptual mapping of precedent case to hypo. By the end of the semester, Jun demonstrates developing control over linking precedent cases to the legal concepts they exemplify and applying those appropriately to a hypothetical fact pattern. Jun has also demonstrated considerable development in conveying the conceptual mapping of the precedent case to hypo to occur at the sentence level.

Case-concept mismatches in Jun's writing were the focus of much of Kurtz's social mediation, and he demonstrates considerable development throughout the semester. Understanding which legal concepts the precedent cases do (and do not) stand for is critical in developing as a legal reasoner. Legal discourse is organized around these concepts (e.g. self-defense) and their sub-concepts (e.g. imminent danger as an element of self-defense) and readers expect this organization. In IRAC 1, Jun selected the appropriate precedent case, but an inappropriate legal concept for the hypo. In IRAC 2, precedent cases were absent from his writing, but when Jun articulated his reason for not engaging with precedent, he and Kurtz engaged in Zone of Proximal Development activity (see Chapter 2) to collaboratively create legal analogies. In IRAC 3, development is

Excerpt 4.7 'No we talk about imminent danger'

1	K	ahm how about imminent danger
2	J	ah i think uh this case should compare with sleeping
3		husband
4	K	mm hmm
5	J	case because in that case a man was sleeping ah it's
6		it's much less imminent danger than this case
7	K	okay
8	J	and in this case is more imminent danger than the
9		sleeping man so i think compare this case this case
10		has imminent danger
11	K	okay so how is the victim in this case more
12		dangerous than the sleeping man
13	J	because he had conscious and he possessing a gun in
14		his hand

demonstrated through the linking of appropriate *mens rea* language for one first-degree murder case and two depraved heart murder cases. And in IRAC 4, further development is demonstrated when Jun organized his entire analysis around Focal Case 4, including the appropriate elements Focal Case 4 analyzed. All of this demonstrates internalization of the concept of legal analogical reasoning and Jun's ability to operate cognitively as a common law *reasoner*.

In writing the IRAC essay, Jun also develops as his analogies become conceptually condensed over time. In IRAC 1, Jun wrote a paragraph about Focal Case 1 and a paragraph about the hypo case but did not conceptually map reasoning from Focal Case 1 onto the hypo. By IRAC 3, Jun has conceptually condensed the entities so that the cases remain discrete at the sentence level and, in his concluding sentence at the level of the noun phrase. This hypo required students to see the legal significance in objects unlikely to be construed as similar in everyday thinking – a loaded gun, two large dogs, and a needle exchange – so the development in the ability to construe the items as legally similar through the categories of homicide is significant. In IRAC 4, Jun still operates at the sentence level rather than intra-sententially, but his analysis contains all of the components of a legal analogy – the legal concept imminent danger is the impetus for the analogy, relevant case facts are compared, and signal language is used to indicate to the reader the relationship between the outcome of the precedent case and the predicted outcome of the hypo. Thus, Jun's analysis develops from treating the cases as discrete entities that receive discrete treatment – multiple sentences each in separate paragraphs – to conceptual and syntactic control to present the precedent case and hypo conceptually in consecutive sentences. This conceptual integration is analogical reasoning development. It is the concise integration of the different entities, a concise mapping of the source domain (precedent case) to target domain (hypo).

Notably in Jun's development, both the social and conceptual mediation appear to have supported Jun's performance and allowed him to externalize still developing capabilities. In the mediation session for IRAC 2, Kurtz and Jun collaboratively complete the thinking process for a legal analogy. Thus, Jun's ability to produce legal analogical reasoning emerges first in collaborative activity before it is observed in independent performance. Likewise, when he used the common law SCOBA to organize analysis of a hypo, Jun produced the thinking for ironic analogies. That is, through the access to conceptual mediation, Jun demonstrated the ability to select appropriate facts to make an argument for both sides. In both instances, the mediation appears to have been appropriately within Jun's Zone of Proximal Development, targeted at ripening abilities and supporting Jun until he can write legal analogies without the use of such support.

5 Graduate Academic Writing: Context, Concepts and Pedagogy

This and the following chapter present Casal's (first author) pedagogical implementation of Concept-Based Language Instruction (C-BLI) in an L2 academic English writing course for graduate students at a large US university (see Casal, 2020, for more details). This project grew out of the needs of the local English for Academic Purposes writing program and graduate students in Casal's context. The graduate writing course for L2 English students was popular, but students represented tremendous diversity in disciplines, such that the course was designed around core linguistic and rhetorical concepts of academic research writing. With this emphasis on using concepts of academic writing to make sense of more localized community practices as the starting point, a course for students across doctoral programs was redesigned around C-BLI and genre-based writing pedagogy. Several linguistic and rhetorical concepts were adopted from L2 writing research as pedagogical foci. This analysis targets shell nouns and rhetorical moves, but other concepts were part of the broader pedagogical intervention and analysis (e.g. reporting verbs). An innovation is that the pedagogical materials are developed based on a large-scale corpus-based genre analysis, and that both personal corpus construction and mediated corpus analysis activities are part of the course activity (collaborative and individual corpus and genre analysis in student developed corpora). Scientific concepts identified in the Second Language Writing and English for Academic Purposes literature are carried into the analysis of linguistic data – first by Casal and later by the students engaged in and mediated through the pedagogy.

Following the aims of C-BLI pedagogies, development is not assessed through changes in student writing alone, but rather through changes in student writers. Student writer development is analyzed across collaborative corpus and genre analysis activities, student conferences, and text protocols with final papers for evidence of developing understanding of target concepts, as well as increased intentionality and principled decision-making in writing and revision.

Pedagogical Context and Participants

The pedagogical intervention took place in a genre-based graduate-level English for Academic Purposes writing course offered at a large US university. Students enroll in this course on an elective basis, typically on their graduate advisor's recommendation. The course focuses on disciplinary academic research-writing genres (research article part-genres, conference abstracts) which are tailored to the student writers' current needs within their programs and disciplines. As part of normal course activity, students write conference abstracts, an introduction/literature review for a research paper, and produce a longer, final text of approximately 20 pages based on their own engagement with disciplinary communities. Prior to developing and teaching this course, Casal was already an experienced instructor of discipline-specific professional and academic English writing instruction, and he had taught the course several times.

Students were recruited from across two sections of the course, and not all enrolled students chose to participate. Participants included 16 doctoral student writers from the following 12 disciplines: Lifelong Learning and Adult Education, Architecture, Architectural Engineering, Chemical Engineering, Ecology, Economics, Electrical Engineering, German Linguistics, Material Science, Mechanical Engineering, Physics, and Political Science. These participants represented Arabic, Chinese, Korean, Portuguese, Russian, and Spanish language backgrounds and 11 countries. Of these 16 participants, 10 were in their last term of course work or first term post–course work, while six were in their second term of course work. All participants had previously met the graduate college's English language proficiency requirements through a TOEFL iBT score of 80 or higher, and many were much more proficient. Participants had varying degrees of publication and presentation experience, but widely identified personal publication and dissertation writing goals, as well as strong pressure from their advisors to develop writing skills.

The Target Concepts

Scientific concepts and corpus linguistics

As has been discussed in Chapter 2, the division between scientific and spontaneous concepts is central to the work of Vygotsky and C-BLI (Lantolf, 2011a). Spontaneous concepts are unsystematic in nature, as they arise from 'generalization of everyday personal experience,' while scientific concepts are systematic in nature and 'represent the generalization of the experience of humankind that is fixed in science' (Karpov, 2003: 65–66). With this in mind, the course curriculum was reshaped around mastery of interfacing rhetorical and linguistic concepts which English for Academic Purposes and Second Language Writing research has identified as key features of academic research writing practices in

English. Instructional content for *concept presentation* and instructional materials for *materialization* phases of class activity were developed based on these rich bodies of scientific research and a large-scale corpus-based genre analysis undertaken by Casal. In this way, the concepts were grounded in extensive research on genre-based writing practices and systematically analyzed in a custom corpus; therefore, they represent the scientific generalization of genre-specific writing practices. Part of class activity also involved collaborative construction (teacher–student) and analysis (teacher–student–student) of corpora reflecting learners' disciplines, which require learners to turn this scientific gaze towards increasingly localized situations of academic writing to reflect on how such decisions are made.

A larger discussion of target concepts and analytical procedures was presented in Casal's unpublished doctoral dissertation (see Casal, 2020), where the methods and findings are reported for a large-scale analysis of shell nouns and rhetorical moves – discussed in this volume – as well as formulaic language, reporting verbs, and syntactically complex structures, which are not discussed in this volume. The target features were analyzed in terms of frequency and functional usage in a corpus of 100 Introduction sections from published research articles each from Applied Linguistics, Economics, Chemical Engineering, and Electrical Engineering. These disciplines were selected to represent the needs of students most commonly enrolled in the target course, while research article introductions were selected based on their prominence in the genre analysis research tradition and by the difficulties that past student writers faced in writing them effectively. They are also a rhetorically complex part of research writing activity that entails the construction of complex intertextual networks and nuanced arguments regarding subject content matter, as well as expression of author positionality and stance. These texts were selected from five top-tier journals from each discipline based on impact factors, distributed evenly across 2012 to 2016 (inclusive). The texts, which are described in Table 5.1, were prepared for corpus analysis by repairing line-split words, manually correcting issues resulting from conversion, and removing elements that were not part of academic prose, as is described in Casal (2020).

Table 5.1 Description of corpus

Discipline	Texts	Total words	Mean words	Words SD	Word range
Applied Ling.	100	61,452	615	413	114–2,565
Chemical Eng.	100	70,978	710	241	225–1,434
Electrical Eng.	100	71,646	716	330	191–2,287
Economics	100	145,633	1,456	480	463–2,846
Total	400	349,709	874	551	114–2,846

Each of the two concepts is briefly introduced, defined, and established as scientific concepts within applied linguistics and writing studies.

Shell nouns

The first concept is a functionally defined linguistic feature, shell nouns (e.g. *fact, idea, problem*), which are an open class of abstract nouns that take a specific meaning from a noun they both index and label in the surrounding discourse (Schmid, 2000). Researchers have long been interested in such words, variably conceptualized as 'general nouns' (Halliday & Hasan, 1976), 'anaphoric nouns' (Francis, 1986), 'carrier nouns' (Ivanič, 1991), 'shell nouns' (Schmid, 2000), 'signaling nouns' (Flowerdew, 2006), and 'metadiscursive nouns' (Jiang & Hyland, 2015), with interest lying in the cognitive, cohesive, and stance-taking dimensions of their use. In this course, shell nouns were taught in order to equip graduate student writers to make careful local decisions regarding how discursive propositions within their texts are labeled and indexed text-internally.

As can be seen in Examples 5.1 and 5.2, shell nouns can reference more elaborate propositions both anaphorically and cataphorically, allowing for emergent, pronoun-like reference. Much research has examined the discursive and cohesive affordances of these resources, and pedagogically they frame a careful attentiveness to how complex concepts are managed within discourse and how much agency a writer has for labeling such concepts.

> Example 5.1: … the **realization** that it was possible to stimulate a prebiotic milieu in the laboratory ushered in a new era in origin-of-life studies. (Flowerdew & Forest, 2015: 1)

> Example 5.2: When propagating through a medium, a pulse of light can travel with a group velocity that is much slower than its vacuum value. **This phenomenon** of slow light has been extensively studied due to its potential for applications ranging from optical buffers to enhanced light-matter interactions (and thus nonlinearity). (Casal, 2020: 155–156)

These examples illustrate how, metaphorically speaking, one could consider *realization* and *phenomenon* to be 'filled' with a specific meaning, such that the terms can be used to invoke the broader concepts succinctly. However, Flowerdew places a strong focus on how these words are not merely 'filled,' as a shell/container metaphor suggests, but also 'label' the proposition they reference. For this reason, Flowerdew uses the term signaling noun (e.g. Flowerdew & Forest, 2015). In Example 5.3, this point is clearly illustrated by the contrasting use of the nouns 'opportunity' and 'problem.'

Example 5.3. *The authors are about to submit their book manuscript for review.*
A. They are eager to take advantage of **this exciting opportunity**.
B. **This problem** has caused them considerable recent anxiety.
(modified from Casal *et al.*, 2024: 4)

The use of such resources has been particularly rich in disciplinary academic writing (e.g. Aktas & Cortes, 2008; Casal *et al.*, 2024; Charles, 2007; Flowerdew & Forest, 2015; Gray, 2010; Gray & Cortes, 2011; Jiang & Hyland, 2015, 2018, 2021; Laso & John, 2013; Schmid, 2000; Wang & Hu, 2023) and first-year and second language writing (Caldwell, 2009; Díez Prados, 2018; Flowerdew, 2006; Hasselgård, 2012; Schanding & Pae, 2018; Sing, 2013). Across many of these studies, '*this/these* + [shell noun]' emerges as a common pattern in academic discourse and a potentially rich site for analyzing learner language. In this study, both the cohesive and labeling functions of these words were taught within this specific linguistic pattern to emphasize how an idea can be agentively repackaged to enhance cohesion and simultaneously further elaborate.

Rhetorical moves

The second concept, rhetorical moves, is not entirely linguistic in nature but strongly frames what writers attempt to accomplish in writing activity. Rhetorical moves, associated with the work of John Swales (e.g. 1981, 1990, 2004), theorize community-specific genre practices as rhetorically staged and recognizable to community members both linguistically and structurally. Move analysis targets the organizational and rhetorical structures that writers use to reach their goals. The analysis entails the development and application of rhetorical move taxonomies that capture broad, recognizable, recurring communicative goals or stages within a text as 'moves,' and more specialized and narrow actions that realize moves as 'steps.' After a move framework is developed, texts are segmented into rhetorical chunks of variable lengths.

Considerable research has adopted rhetorical move analysis to profile the rhetorical decisions disciplinary writers make within and across fields in abstracts (e.g. Hyland, 2000; Lorés, 2004; Pho, 2008; Samraj, 2005; Santos, 1996; Tankó, 2017; Yoon & Casal, 2020a), research article introductions (e.g. Hirano, 2009; Samraj, 2002; Soler-Monreal *et al.*, 2011), literature reviews (e.g. Jian, 2010; Kwan *et al.*, 2012), as well as results and/or discussion sections (e.g. Basturkmen, 2009, 2011; Bruce, 2009; Parkinson, 2011; Yang & Allison, 2003). Many move analysis studies and pedagogical applications of move-based genre analysis have, like this one, integrated corpus-based investigation of formal linguistic features with discourse-based examination of rhetorical stages to examine how writers mobilize linguistic resources to signal rhetorical goals (Casal &

Kessler, 2020; Cortes, 2013; Durrant & Mathews-Aydınlı, 2011; Gray *et al.*, 2020; Le & Harrington, 2015; Liu & Lu, 2020; Lu *et al.*, 2020; Omidian *et al.*, 2018; Yoon & Casal, 2020b). Perhaps the most wellknown rhetorical move framework is the Creating a Research Space model (Swales, 1990), which describes recurring rhetorical activities in empirical research papers across many disciplines.

Before developing the course content, Casal conducted a rhetorical move analysis of the 400-text disciplinary corpus to develop pedagogical materials and deepen his own conceptual understanding. Students engaged in rhetorical move analysis of texts in their own personal corpora of texts within their disciplines, both collaboratively and individually. The rhetorical move framework used in this study and the analytical procedures of its applications are described in considerable depth in Casal (2020). In summary, the move framework was developed collaboratively by a team of seven writing specialists as part of a series of studies (e.g. Lu *et al.*, 2018, 2020). Small adaptations were made to reflect the inclusion of Engineering (the final framework is presented in Table 5.2). Coding procedures for Applied Linguistics and Economics yielded high reliability (Cohen's Kappa 0.81), Casal applied the same protocols to the

Table 5.2 Rhetorical move framework for research article introductions

Move/step	Name
Move 1	**Establishing a research territory**
Step 1A	Claiming scholarly centrality of research area
Step 1B	Claiming real-world centrality of research area
Step 2	Generalizing about research area
Step 3	Reviewing items of previous research
Move 2	**Establishing a niche**
Step 1A	Problematizing previous research/practice
Step 1B	Indicating a gap
Step 1C	Question-raising
Step 1D	Continuing a tradition
Step 2	Providing justification for filling gap
Move 3	**Presenting the present work**
Step 1	Announcing present research
Step 2	Presenting research questions or hypotheses
Step 3	Definitional clarification
Step 4	Summarizing methods
Step 5	Preview outcomes
Step 6	Stating the value of the present research
Step 7	Rationalizing research focus and design
Step 8	Outlining the structure of the paper

Engineering data, and inter-coder reliability with a paid writing specialist research assistant who coded 42 of these texts was high (Cohen's Kappa 0.84).

Description of Pedagogy and Data Sources

Learners were each mediated through the construction of a personal corpus (see Charles, 2024) of research articles within their disciplines in journals that they hoped to publish in (henceforth *personal corpora*). In Casal (2020), attention is dedicated to the rich space for introspection and imagined identity afforded by this activity, as a rich corpus construction culture emerged around learners' considering carefully which papers to include as data. These corpora were shared with Casal for collaborative reference, so that he could pull sample texts from across disciplines for class activities. The corpus that the researcher had previously analyzed was also used at times (henceforth *general corpus*).

The course itself was designed based on C-BLI, which targets the development of explicit conceptual knowledge as 'both the content and the tool for thinking' (Negueruela, 2008: 192) in practical, application-based activity. Overall, class activities progressed through the following stages: (a) instructor led introduction of scientific concepts with an emphasis on explicit, systematic knowledge development through *concept presentation* and *materialization*, (b) instructor-mediated group-based rhetorical/discourse analysis and general corpus analysis text-focused activities which aim to bridge the abstract concepts to concrete activity and encourage *verbalization/languaging*, (c) instructor-mediated individual rhetorical/discourse analysis and personal corpus analysis activities which localize the concepts to more immediate target domains and encourage *verbalization*, (d) group discussion of findings to promote *verbalization* and create additional opportunities for mediation, (e) engagement in discipline specific writing discussion and activity supported by instructor conferences to promote *verbalization* and mediate engagement in disciplinary writing tasks, and (f) various reflective activities to further promote *verbalization* and introspection while contributing to the instructor–student relationship.

Concept Presentation was motivated by the development of schematic knowledge of scientific concepts explicitly and led to the introduction of materialized artifacts. Linguistic and rhetorical concepts were presented to learners explicitly through definitions, explicit grammatical explanations in the case of shell nouns, discussion of functional affordances, description of taxonomies and frameworks as presented in the previous concept overview section, and discussion of examples in context. Examples were all drawn from the corpus-based genre analysis that Casal carried out on the general corpus and represented a range of patterns. Materializations were diverse and took the form of annotated texts, linguistic examples, illustrations, and visualizations that were marked up to create physical learning tools. Learners were encouraged to (and often asked to) create visual representations of target concepts. Some of them, such as Figure 5.1 on shell nouns, were taken up by classmates for reference in collaborative interthinking (Mercer, 2000), serving as mediational resources and shared artifacts. In Figure 5.1, the image on the left illustrates the cohesive function of shell nouns, as three distinct ideas are placed within a box labeled problems. This also underscores the repackaging and labeling function of shell nouns, with repackaging in particular entering the shared classroom metalanguage when the student authors share this, instead of when Casal introduced it. The right side of the image shows the writer carrying the box of problems and handing it to a reader, with a linguistic illustration below exemplifying the discursive activity represented.

These concepts were then the basis of genre analysis and corpus analysis activities in large group, small group, and individual settings that targeted reflections on the structures, their potential affordances, and writer decisions. Building on Charles's (2007, 2011) work, many class activities involved corpus-based language analysis (mediated data-driven learning) and textual analysis as 'two equally important elements' (Charles, 2011: 28) in reinforcing iteration. Text analysis activities required learners to use course artifacts and conceptual understandings to identify and interpret target features in context, reflect on and weigh alternatives, and verbalize both their rationales for conclusions drawn and evolving

Figure 5.1 Student-produced visualization of shell nouns

understanding of concepts. Corpus analysis activities brought a focus to the patterns and range of resources that writers use to accomplish predictable goals and allowed the class to challenge assumptions and conclusions that arose from analyzing small datasets in text analysis. Corpus analysis for rhetorical moves made use of move-tagged texts in the general corpus. All activities foregrounded both prototypical patterns and creative instances to frame decision-making around the concept and within the dialectic relationship that exists between creativity and convention in genre. These activities extend the development of conceptual knowledge by instantiating it in concrete activity and localizing the conceptual resources to more defined activities and disciplinary domains. There is a move from equipping learners with a materialized and mediated basis for orienting to class activity to 'grasping' the concept in a procedural manner to abstracting a flexible and functional understanding and aiming to promote verbalization to push learners away from reliance on course artifacts themselves (Lantolf & Poehner, 2014). These tasks are also connected with more personal and practical writing activities, which included conferences with Casal, work on individual major writing projects, revision activities, and various planning and reflection tasks.

Throughout all pedagogical activities, the social and situated nature of genre practices was emphasized, as was the tension between convention and choice in academic writing (Tardy, 2016), with learners encouraged to reflect on their own participation in disciplinary activity out of class. AntConc (Anthony, 2019) was used for all corpus analysis activities. Casal provided considerable training and support in the use of AntConc, including in-class instructional activities, tutorial videos, and extra workshops for each activity. Formal and rhetorical features or characteristics of genre practices are presented and considered as inextricably connected and co-emergent in highly specialized disciplinary contexts, rather than as isolated inventories and skills. This is practically enacted through integrated corpus and genre analysis activities, such as those discussed in Charles (2007, 2011), which emphasize both how discourse and rhetoric are built up locally from highly variable textual elements but are also notably conventionalized across texts. For this reason, neither corpus-based nor genre analysis–based pedagogical activities took precedence over the other, but rather they were integrated iteratively where macro-level corpus-deduced patterns were instantiated and challenged in local textual contexts, and discourse analysis–based observations are reinforced and extended through macro-level pattern analysis. This emphasizes the genre practice and the linguistic-rhetorical concepts rather than the conventions themselves, and it frames decision-making in academic writing as a local decision made with various competing goals and implications in mind, rather than a formula, checklist, or rule of thumb. Genre serves as a metacognitive frame for disciplinary writing activity, such that learners are acquiring new ways for thinking about and engaging with writing tasks, and they are internalizing and appropriating new psychological resources for navigating such spaces. From a C-BLI perspective, the appropriation of specific linguistic (e.g. shell nouns) and rhetorical (e.g. rhetorical moves) concepts through which learners can think while agentively engaged in such activity is the object of the intervention.

As with the other interventions in this volume, Casal adopted a responsive mediator (Johnson & Golombek, 2016) role, dynamically engaging students with variable assistance ranging from implicit to explicit as deemed appropriate for their moment-to-moment potentiality (Aljaafreh & Lantolf, 1994). In this regard, more implicit assistance may involve directing attention or encouraging introspection, intermediate forms may include reminding a learner of a mediational resource or pedagogical concept, and more explicit forms include providing partial and complete answers. The pedagogical intervention revolved around opportunities for student writers to develop and apply explicit conceptual knowledge of target linguistic and rhetorical resources; apply their knowledge of and explore, reflect on, and experiment with such resources; use these resources to *write*; and verbalize their decision-making processes and understandings. Such a sociocultural and genre-based approach targets development through the internalization of psychological tools and resources rather than accumulation of isolated *pieces of knowledge*.

Data was collected from multiple sources, including samples of student writing (a research article introduction draft and later revisions within the whole research article), eight audio-recorded class meetings which include class-wide discussions and group activities, and 45-minute individual semi-structured text-protocols targeting writers' linguistic and rhetorical decisions in the drafting and revision of their final text.

Students enrolled in the course identify a major writing task that they are working on as part of their engagement with disciplinary and pedagogical activity, and the tasks are tailored to their particular needs and aims. All but three graduate student participants of this study aimed to produce a research article text for submission to a scholarly journal through course activity. Two were working on other research-related disciplinary tasks (a detailed summary of their dissertation for a fellowship application and a conference proceedings chapter), while the other student was writing a standalone literature review for the course. For this reason, student participants submitted a draft of an introduction mid-way through the pedagogical intervention (after eight weeks of instruction) and a final version at the end of the semester as part of their final submission. The guidelines were tailored to the individual learners and their disciplinary context, as student writers were asked to identify a specific journal and follow the requirements, conventions, and guidelines for authors for that particular journal. Extensive feedback was provided on the first draft, and learners also submitted smaller tasks (e.g. conference abstracts and grant proposals) variably as they related to their disciplinary activity, all receiving feedback from Casal. Students frequently interacted with Casal in future-focused (rather than evaluative) conferences on writing where an emphasis was placed on externalizing aims and rationales in addition to grammatical concerns. Learners were asked to include a two-page reflection on how they have developed as writers during the term with their final paper submission with specific reference to the course activities and concepts. These texts were also included in the analysis for participants. While participants all agreed that their writing could be collected and analyzed by Casal, students were told that no portion of their research writing would be reproduced in written form due to the ongoing nature of their scholarship, funding sources, and/or advisor requests.

Eight 75-minute course meetings were also audio-recorded in the first two-thirds of the 16-week course. The course met twice a week, and both class meetings were recorded in Weeks 3, 4, 6, and 9, to target pedagogical activities that prominently featured the linguistic and rhetorical constructs in focus during phase one and the concept-based and integrated corpus and genre analysis activities over time. As learners worked regularly in smaller groups formed loosely around disciplines, microphones were placed in front of Casal and next to participating groups by a research assistant. Zoom H1 Handy Recorder microphones were used for these recordings, as the high-quality multi-directional microphones and directional speaker identification facilitated the transcription process.

All participants also met with Casal for individual 45–60 minute text-based interview sessions to discuss the writing and revision of the final research article text for submission in Week 16, with a particular emphasis on learners' decision-making processes and intentionality. Similar text protocol meetings have been used in other scholarship to 'provoke explicit writer comments relating to noticing and language awareness' (Lindgren & Sullivan, 2003: 172). Text protocols relate more broadly to work in the sociocultural tradition of language teacher education that leverages the mediated activity of retroactive reconstruction and reflection to provide insights into participants' orientation to goal-directed activity, conceptual development, and as a mediational means of development itself. These meetings serve as a primary data source for exploring learners' appropriation of course concepts as resources for thinking about and engaging with writing-based disciplinary activity.

These meetings were conducted throughout the semester, but they were recorded in the 14th and 15th week of the 16-week course with the final draft. They were staged and semi-structured in nature. The text protocols were dynamic, they proceeded roughly as follows. First, participants were asked to briefly explain their topic to the interviewer and to explicate the rhetorical construction of the Introduction section of the text. During this stage, the interviewer occupied the role of a responsive mediator and encouraged the participant to verbalize their rationale for their decisions. In many cases, the participants voluntarily discussed their revisions with the interviewer, as the interviewer was familiar with previous drafts. In other cases, the interviewer prompted the participants to discuss their revisions from previous submissions. Before moving to the second stage, the interviewer asked the participants to explain other rhetorical structures and organizational options they may have considered and why they avoided them. In stage two, the interviewer prompted the participants to indicate specific linguistic features that they had integrated to signal their rhetorical aims. Similar to the first stage, the interviewer asked the participants to explain their revisions, rationales, and alternatives that they considered. During the third stage of these text protocols, the interviewer provided the participants an open-ended opportunity to discuss other writing-based considerations that they would like to share regarding the construction and revision of the text, after which the interviewer prompted the participants to reflect on particular rhetorical, formal linguistic features, and revisions that were deemed salient but had not been discussed.

Analytical Procedures

Data is analyzed with two primary goals: to provide insights into the experiences of the learners engaged in this pedagogical activity and to assess the impacts of the pedagogy on L2 graduate student research article introduction genre knowledge through a genetic conceptualization of development (Lantolf & Thorne, 2006). After the pedagogical intervention was completed, Casal reviewed the various sources of data chronologically to develop a holistic, cross-participant horizon of developmental trajectories and experiences. Casal then reviewed all the data for each participant individually, analyzing learners' response to the pedagogical intervention and how the development of conceptual genre knowledge for engaging in academic research writing activity arose through evidence of (a) explicit knowledge of concept through the ability to discuss concepts through course materials/with instructor mediation and identify instances of structures, (b) more developed and abstract systematic knowledge of concept through the ability to verbalize such understandings more independently and discuss writer intentions, (c) appropriative control of concept through the ability to verbalize intentionality and principled reasoning in writing choices and class activity, (d) more developed appropriative control and conceptual self-regulation through flexible application and transfer of concepts to novel domains or integration of conceptual resources, and (e) changes in learner writing itself, which is important for showing the 'effectiveness' of the pedagogy in a broader educational world.

During this process, segments of classroom recordings and text protocols were transcribed through verbatim transcription by Casal both as a means of preparing the data for systematic analysis and presentation, and as a means of analysis itself. Transcriptions only broadly captured pauses and tone contours, mostly to mark interrogative statements. Gestures and gaze are not included, as this data source was audio-recorded. For these three learners, all recorded data was transcribed by Casal through verbatim transcription with minimal marking of pauses, gestures, and tones. Throughout this analytical activity, Casal considered the windows into student conceptual development with the understanding that such introspective activity is simultaneously interventional and mediational. That is to say that the student experiences and development of conceptual resources cannot be fully divorced from the mediated site in which it took place, from the mediational role of Casal, or from the rich sociocultural and disciplinary histories of the graduate student participants.

6 Graduate Academic Writing: Findings and Implications

This chapter presents a portion of Casal's analysis of how a Concept-Based Genre Writing pedagogy impacted graduate student multilingual writers' development of conceptual and genre knowledge over the 16-week pedagogical intervention in an academic writing course at a large US university. C-BLI is a transformational pedagogy, so while schematic knowledge of target concepts is essential, as is the mediational means through which that knowledge is developed, this chapter places a more overt focus on how orientation to and engagement with the genre practice is transformed through internalization of target concepts. That is, in this chapter, a primary focus is on changes in graduate student writers' stance toward target concepts and the genre practices the class is projected toward, with primary emphasis on evidence that learners are engaging in new ways of thinking about academic research writing and making more intentional and agentive decisions. Of the 16 doctoral student participants, most showed considerable growth in the development of their conceptual knowledge of shell nouns and rhetorical moves (as well as other concepts not covered here), their awareness of the academic research writing as a purpose-driven community-specific genre practice, and their ability to think about, talk about, and engage with academic research writing in novel ways. Other students demonstrated a growing understanding of target concepts in the context of classroom activities and definitional verbalizations but limited ability to utilize such knowledge when making decisions in their own writing. Developmental trajectories were diverse, individual, and non-linear.

Further analysis is presented in Casal (2020), an unpublished doctoral dissertation, where emphasis is placed on more concepts in greater detail, as well as the internalization of conceptual knowledge itself. This chapter presents a case-study analysis of two doctoral student participants' developmental trajectories (Mona and Lucía, pseudonyms) to provide insights into how the new psychological tools they gained through the Concept-Based Genre Writing pedagogy transformed how they think about academic research writing.

As a note on transcriptions, transcribed excerpts from pair work and instructor–student interactions are presented with the following broad transcription conventions for the remainder of this chapter:

[beginning of overlapping speech
() gesture, laughter, or other descriptive text
? rising intonation suggesting a question
+ short pause
CAPS   emphasis
T   Casal (Author 1)
(()) redacted content (e.g. student name; confidential information)

Mona: Agency and Autonomy through Resistance and Creativity

Mona was a second-semester doctoral student in Lifelong Learning and Adult Education who had recently transitioned from a career as an engineer after her experiences with social movements, protests, and revolution in her home country. She viewed her PhD as a means of acquiring the cultural capital, theoretical resources, and personal strength necessary to return home and enact education-based reform. Mona was working closely with her advisor to compose innovative scholarly autoethnographic contributions to her field, and she was deeply invested in improving her academic writing skills to get her papers published and her ideas out in the world. Her professional goals were closely tied to personal convictions, creating a strong investment in learning that at times manifested itself as resistance to new topics, but also allowed her to eventually bridge course concepts with her own personal and disciplinary goals through the frames and currents of genre practices, as is intended by the pedagogy. This is not to say that she mastered all target concepts.

Based on Mona's start of term reflections on her writing strengths, writing weaknesses, and goals for the course, her initial understanding of her own writing was that it was '*in good shape*,' but she needed this course to '*clean up grammatical issues and improve clarity*.' Nevertheless, Mona reported feeling '*alienated from academic writing*,' framing her writing process as '*a long journey filled with suffering*' and '*like torture*.' She felt guilt and shame for not writing more often and pressure from the growing weight of writing projects. She also expressed and demonstrated strong investment in improving through the course. Mona's emphasis on *grammar* as the pathway to better writing is neither surprising nor unique, but it provides insights into the nature of her orientation to writing activity as grammatical, clear, and factual, as well as something experienced, rather than an agentive activity. Mona did not demonstrate an initial understanding of the rhetorical nature of research writing broadly or through scientific concepts relevant to writing.

Advancing into the semester, Mona's orientation to *writing as grammar* was profound, such that she resisted as an expression of the perceived misalignment between her aims and her understanding of course activity during concept presentations. This resistance was never disruptive in practice or intention, rather it took the form of jokes, requests for 'answers,' and reminders that she had deadlines and high-stakes writing tasks that needed to improve quickly. Excerpt 6.1 presents an early example of these tensions. She worked with her partner to complete a series of tasks that required students to use their explicit understandings of shell nouns and pedagogical materials to identify shell nouns in context, reflect on their usage for cohesion, and reflect on the 'signaling' and 'repackaging' function of shell nouns (Flowerdew & Forest, 2015). At the start of Excerpt 6.1, Mona (M) and her partner (S1, from the same discipline) move on to a corpus activity to consider a broader range of shell nouns and contexts and the diversity of stances writers adopt in local discourse contexts. Mona alternates between working collaboratively with her partner on the task and orienting away from the task to make jokes or comments on the activities and course themselves. These comments often reveal a struggle to reconcile the novel scientific concepts with her own spontaneous understanding of writing as grammar and content knowledge.

While her partner begins to interact with the corpus through AntConc (Anthony, 2019), Mona orients toward her partner but away from the task in line 1. Her tone, as captured through the audio recording, is friendly but mocking, as she reflects on how the text and corpus analysis activities allow her to see what the target features afford in context, but that she cannot yet take them up herself. While this is hypothesized through a Vygotskian approach to development, Mona frames this as a flaw in the design, also noting (in lines 6 and 7) that Casal's concept presentation renders the concept understandable, but she frames it as misleading. Likewise, in line 2 Mona discusses shell noun use as a formula, which is antithetical to the pedagogy, and in the final line she teasingly calls her partner by the instructor's name to playfully mock the supportive nature of the pedagogy.

And yet we also see Mona engaging with the task in a manner that displays developing understanding of the shell noun concept. When her partner identifies an instance in line 9 and focuses on the formal aspect (e.g. '*how can the writer use two*'), Mona reproduces metalanguage from the concept presentation and class materials (lines 20–21) and properly conceptualizes the shell noun concept as something you do with a word rather than an intrinsic principle of a word. While her partner is more demonstratively *on task*, it is Mona's thinking and understanding of the important components of shellnounhood that direct them through the task and keep the notions of stance and cohesion in focus above forms.

Excerpt 6.1 Week four – Student group work on shell nouns

1	M:	yeah see? writing is easy[(laughs)
2	S1:	[writing is easy (laughs)
3	M:	the thing is that when I read these phrases it is easy + its like oh yeah one
4		plus one equals two just take this sentence + explain it that way but when
5		I write it + its not like that (laughs) yeah
6	S1:	(laughs) yeah
7	M:	like + when he simplifies it + OH + that like + woah + sounds like +
8		how come I'm not doing that?
9	S1:	(mumbles) this + problem
10	M:	its like if I understood how to make that kind of sentence
11	S1:	I think that maybe we have a problem [(laughs)
12	M:	[we have a screen full of problems
13	S1:	this one is interesting + in THESE examples THIS problem?
14	M:	click + click it? + these examples + that's a good one + I named one
15	S1:	you're good + you don't need to take this class (laughs)
16	M:	(laughs) I think maybe yes
17	S1:	how can the writer use two + use both
18	M:	it is like a pro [pronoun
19	S1:	[pronoun + right
20	M:	a shell noun can refer to another idea like a pronoun + repackage an idea
21		to build on later + here it must refer back to examples and problems
22	S1:	you + you + you think that EXAMPLE is a? + can be a?
23	M:	include both example + NO because it needs to refer to something before
24		that so it needs[to
25	S1:	yeah example + example is a lot + yeah before + look [at these up here
26	M:	ah yeah yeah [I'm thinking
27	S1:	[here here
28	M:	do you think it is?
29	S1:	yeah + case and example is similar + right?
30	M:	ah + mmmm + but I feel that example is more tangible and if we look
31		shell noun implied repackaging the idea
32	S1:	ah you are good (laughs)
33	M:	thank you Elliott (laughs)

In this and other group tasks in the early weeks, Mona embraces opportunities to express her preferences for more traditional approaches to grammar or otherwise resist, but she also demonstrates an ability to work with target concepts with an expected degree of external mediation at this early stage of contact with the concepts. During these weeks, Mona struggled between a conceptualization of academic research writing as primarily subject-domain knowledge plus grammatical accuracy and a pedagogy that framed writing around choice and agency. Mona approached class activities as disjointed '*English lessons,*' and was initially unable to connect course content to her own decision-making in writing, preferring to '*take up*' example words she liked and drop them in her text. At the same time, through foregrounding verbalization and agency, the pedagogy frames an explicit space for the dissonance between her pre-understanding and the scientific concepts to play out.

A sharp change in Mona's stance can be observed in Except 6.2, which occurred in week 6 and persisted. While Mona had demonstrated a similar explicit understanding of rhetorical moves as displayed in Excerpt 6.1 regarding shell nouns, such knowledge and noticing the features in context did not prompt her to navigate her own research writing through the lens of these conceptual tools. During this task, with her growing understanding of rhetorical moves and the stance-taking affordances of shell nouns (and other features) in a pedagogical space which is structured around her agency and continuously pushing her to externalize, Mona takes a major step in moving past her initial orientation to grammar and recognizes, through the course concepts, academic research writing as a situational social practice.

Excerpt 6.2 Week six – Student group work

1	T:	how are you guys [do
2	M:	honestly [great but + everything is a move + is that + is +
3	S1:	[good yeah
4	T:	(laughs) everything?
5	M:	I mean there are all these things that the writer is trying to do
6	T:	yeah aside from just presenting facts about the research
7	M:	yeah
8	T:	and where do + where do you guys see that? for example
9	M:	ok (long pause) like here she says this gap is surprising
10		considering that + and it is the m + the move two step two
11	T:	which one is that
12	M:	the one after gap + its called rationalizing
13	T:	I agree with you guys + and that is an important rhetorical move +
14		why do you + why do you think that they need that
15	M:	+ it sounds academic [(laughs)
16	T:	[it sounds academic? (laughs)
17	S1:	[(laughs) I think maybe + maybe +
18	T:	yeah? ((says name))?
19	S1:	well its just that we talked about how not all gaps are worth addressing
20		so I thought that maybe in our field this sort of question isn't common
21		+ and the writer + tries [to m
22	M:	[oh that's good this is + this is good
23	T:	(laughs) what is it?
24	M:	I + you are right + she is saying + like + ok so we haven't looked at this
25		question before and that's ok but THIS is why it is important that we do
26	S1:	exactly + I + yeah that's what +
27	T:	That's what I see the writer doing too + and you can see why it may be
28		important to say that sometimes [+ and + how did you decide that move
29	S1:	[I do
30	M:	[for sure (laughs)
31	M:	oh we saw the + gap is surprising + and it + whats the word you used? +
32		trigger? + it was a trigger
33	T:	yeah + or a signal + or a cue + they all work + I think trigger in the book
34	M:	at first I thought it was just saying this is my gap but its subtle
35	S1:	shell + shell noun + this gap is surprising
36	T:	right + it all piles [up (laughs)
37	M:	its everywhere (laughs)

Excerpt 6.2 begins with Casal showing up, whereby Mona greets him with the realization that *'everything is a move'* (line 2) and that *'there are all these things that the writer is trying to do'* (line 5). Casal had interpreted her prior resistance as an expression of cognitive dissonance between her pre-understanding of good academic writing, the scientific concepts, and the pedagogy, and in line 6 he responds by placing her new comments in contrast to her prior views (i.e. that writing was exclusively *factual*), and prompts her to explain the rationale for her claim in line 8, which is a strategy continued in lines 11, 14, and 28.

Mona and her partner had identified in the text a rather strong rhetorical signal (*'this gap is surprising, considering that'*) and determined that the author was not only building space for their study, but showing why it was important to address the gap. Mona is able to identify the move using the physical rhetorical move framework she has printed out, but she is initially unable to verbalize a principled reason for why an author may engage in such rhetorical activity, instead claiming that it *'sounds academic'* (line 15). Her partner uses language from the concept presentation and course materials in offering a more socially aware response (lines 19–21), which prompts Mona to eagerly announce her agreement in an apparent epiphany. She demonstrates an ability to recast the writer's rhetorical aims in her own schematic frame (lines 24 and 25), rather than read the move description from the sheet, exclaiming *'so we haven't looked at this question before and that's ok but THIS is why it is important that we do.'* Taking up the academic language of the text, linking it to a rhetorical move in the framework, and recasting it in her own words suggests access to the concept in the emerging interactional space through colloquialized communicative verbalization. Mona then searches for the metalanguage used to label the linguistic chunk and produces a term which was used in a class reading, bringing her emerging conceptualization in line with the course metalanguage used for the scientific concept. She is also intellectually excited about her discovery, repeating that *'this is good'* to herself in line 22 and proclaiming that rhetoric is *'everywhere'* in the final line.

At the time, Casal cautiously interpreted this as early evidence of a reorientation to academic writing through acceptance of the scientific concept of rhetorical moves and a recognition that writing was social and rhetorical. A few days later Mona resubmitted her conference abstract that was substantially revised to closely follow the rhetorical move framework for conference abstracts in Yoon and Casal (2020a). While the revisions demonstrated a rather close implementation of the framework, the revisions mark a positive reorientation toward course content through a willingness to connect her work with class discussions. In terms of concept development, this also demonstrates Mona engaging in new ways of thinking about writing (and new ways of writing) through the rhetorical moves concept.

Advancing to her major writing assignment, Mona submitted two drafts of the introduction and literature review for a major paper she was working on for publication with her advisor as second author. Excerpts 6.3 and 6.4 are from a text protocol meeting with Casal at the end of the term to discuss her decision-making for the draft in its current form and to discuss a future writing plan.

As can be seen in Excerpt 6.3, Mona self-reported the largest improvement in her ability to recognize target concepts in other academic reading. For example, in lines 3 through 6 she articulates a reorientation to genre practices through the realization that writers reveal their attitudes and '*show their identities*' in writing practices, and likewise she demonstrates an ability to transfer and apply this discovery to other genres (i.e. term papers) and imagine the perspectives of professor readers. In a sharp contrast to her pre-understanding of writing as grammatical, clear, and factual, she now foregrounds reader perception and writer identity. Similarly, she externalizes a developing understanding of genre as composed of intertwined rhetorical and formal domains (line 9). She exemplifies this understanding in lines 11 through 14 by identifying a purpose for reading (i.e. skimming) and how her understanding of interconnected formal and functional concepts may facilitate such activity. In line 18, she says about many target and ancillary concepts from class '*I see them and it is very conscious . . . and I name them,*' explicitly articulating that the scientific concept and surrounding metalanguage interface with and mediate her reading in a conscious manner.

These are Mona's descriptions of her development, but through them we can see that her thinking about writing has shifted profoundly from mechanics and subject content to include notions of *self*, of *showing*, and of *audience*, connected to stance and rhetoric. When Mona is asked to explain the rhetorical structure of her revised final text, a different sort of evidence emerges. In Excerpt 6.4, Mona discusses the considerable revisions she made to her final paper. She begins with an explanation of her motivation, strongly demonstrating enhanced feelings of control and agency in writing, as well as a developed understanding of rhetorical framing as an expression of authorial voice in relation to her goals. This is a considerable development from writing '*torture*' inflicted on her or her rationale in week 6 (see Excerpt 6.2) that rhetorical moves are important because they '*sound academic.*' She references both the purpose of her text and her awareness of how a particular non-standard reader demographic for research articles may react to a more traditional academic text, signaling increased awareness of the intersecting components of genre introduced in the course (community context, communicative purpose, recognizable form).

In an innovative application of her understanding of rhetorical moves, she explains in lines 5–7, 11–16, and 23–27 that she deconstructed a poem that was prominent as a song to the protests which her work

Excerpt 6.3 Text protocol with Mona

1	M:	after analyzing the way that moves and all the language parts we talked
2		about + are working together in texts I really started to pay attention
3		when reading + and + and realized that when authors are expressing their
4		ideas they also express their attitudes and show their identities + so it is
5		very scary to think to know that I never thought about what I was
6		showing in my writing and I think that is probably something that
7		professors can see when they read our work + you know? + so now I can
8		see that the ideas and the language and the + rhetoric are all mixed and
9		connected to each other (draws outstretched fingers together in a point)
10	T:	right
11	M:	for example I can go for the gist of the paper by checking the bundles that
12		are showing the moves that are related to the announcement of the goals +
13		and purposes of the work and these days I know what is the difference
14		between READING + and SKIMMING.
15	T:	right right + and [you
16	M:	[and that is where I see it is in the reading + sorry in the
17		reading + I feel very confident and proud because I NOTICE these things
18		+ I see them and it is very conscious + and I name them + shell noun +
19		gap + look look at that really long noun phrase + oh maybe that's a
20		frame?
21	T:	and with writing?
22	M:	+ (tilts head) yeah + with writing + with writing I am MORE conscious
23		too + but I don't know + of course + if what I am + if what I am writing is
24		good you know? my advisor likes it (laughs) but also gives me lots of
25		feedback

responds to and used distinct verses as signals of her rhetorical aims; each line on its own announced the rhetorical aim of a section (e.g. territory; motivation) creatively. This was not done purely as an act of creativity, but with the intentional, principled aim of rendering her work less opaque to the non-academic reader demographics she hoped her work could benefit. This represents the ability to think through the concepts of rhetorical moves in academic writing to deconstruct non-academic text and use it to reconstruct academic text; it is appropriatively applying a concept to both enact and innovate a genre convention within her discipline in order to advance a specific set of objectives with a diverse audience in mind. From a C-BLI perspective, this points toward a fairly developed conceptual understanding of rhetorical moves and suggests that Mona is beginning to use rhetoric and rhetorical moves and signals as psychological tools for making meaning in writing-based disciplinary activity. From a genre-based perspective, this is an impressive step forward in her awareness of her own aims in relation to the social practices and situations she is engaging in.

In the final lines of this brief excerpt from the interaction, Mona returns to the issue of grammar, admitting to Casal that she still thinks it is important, but not in the same way as she had previously. Here she once more utilizes her conceptual understanding of rhetoric to solve a

Excerpt 6.4 Text protocol with Mona

```
1   M:   when I started this I didn't want this to be a serious academic paper so
2        + because of the purpose and the audience also includes + teachers + it
3        is also for teachers
4   T:   ok
5   M:   so I decided to use this poem + its its + one of the most important +
6        famous poems that we used during the movement and it addresses the
7        topic + in this way
8   T:   oh that is an interesting idea + and how did you decide to use it this way
9   M:   you always ask that (laughs)
10  T:   I (laughs) I know + sorry
11  M:   (laughs) so I decided to use verses from the poem to structure the whole
12       paper which was an idea that I got from + from the idea of rhetorical
13       moves (laughs) actually + which maybe isn't right + but I saw the
14       different stages that I would want in my paper in the poem + the context
15       and its importance to society + the need that it addresses + the purpose of
16       my + the study + and even + method + methods
17  T:   so even songs have academic moves in them?
18  M:   (laughs) that (laughs)
19  T:   sorry (laughs) I'm just kidding
20  M:   so I think this works
21  T:   when reading this last night I thought that you did it that way + but then I
22       doubted myself + I thought + you've been reading too many papers
23  M:   no no + you are true + right + that is what I tried to do + I was thinking +
24       ok ok + so I have this paper that I am writing for my audience + and my I
25       am trying to ((redacted; states papers aim)) + but there are other stages of
26       my paper and the readers may not all be familiar with academic papers +
27       so so + I wanted to make these things clear
28  T:   do [you think
29  M:        [at the beginning + sorry + I have to say at the beginning I thought it
30       was the grammar + I really did + and he was like + my advisor + I don't
31       think I have an issue with YOUR grammar + and I don't have issue with +
32       and he was like always encouraging me that + your structure or your ideas
33       is really good + which was kind of like (puts hand on heart) + but he said
34       that I wasn't + the word was always CLEAR
35  T:   that's the word
36  M:   it was + and you know + I think its grammar too (laughs) but I think it was
37       rhetoric + I didn't have rhetorical aims (laughs) seriously + and when I did
38       they weren't signaled
39  T:   right + so how does that relate to clarity + in your view?
40  M:   the reader has to figure it out + I ignored them + just talking about myself
```

novel problem, unpacking the meaning of clarity, a key concept for her pre-understanding. She suggests that her advisor's issues with her work were not due to a lack of clarity caused by grammatical issues, as she once believed, but by rhetorical issues. Mona suggests that it was difficult for readers to deduce what she was attempting to accomplish in her writing, because she herself was not aware. Mona comes to this realization through the scientific concept of rhetorical moves, summed up in an insightful characterization of a novice writer's mentality: '*I ignored them, just talking about myself*,' with 'them' referring to her readers. In this sense, Mona has also used the rhetorical move concept to make sense of her discarded pre-understanding.

Lucía: Scrutiny, Playfulness and Innovation

Lucía was a second-year PhD student in Ecology, and her aim for enrolling in the course being to '*get [her] dissertation proposal done*' highlights her sharp pragmatism. She had a clear aim of becoming a professor, either in the United States or in her home nation, and so she maintained interests in scholarly research communities in both English and her L1. Lucía was younger than many of her classmates, but also the most accomplished with publication. Her commitment to improving her academic writing skills were practically driven by her ambitious career goals and encouraged by her supportive advisor. She was engaged, reflective, and productively skeptical; her openness and open-mindedness proved to be valuable assets, as Lucía demonstrated a unique ability to adapt course concepts to her domain, rapidly integrate and appropriate them, and develop catchy metalanguage that amused and mediated her classmates.

Like Mona, Lucía was a skeptical class participant from the beginning, but her skepticism was neither disaffiliative nor temporary. Lucía openly stated her reservations to novel course concepts, experimented with them, and readily announced changes in her opinions. As soon as the third day of class, Lucía provided an example of this sort of disposition in response to another student's question. When discussing shell nouns and cohesion (Excerpt 6.5), a learner points out that there is value in '*repetition*' of words too. The instructor agrees (line 2), and Lucía immediately raises her hand to challenge.

As can be seen in lines 6–8, Lucía expresses friendly skepticism at the idea that repetition contributes to cohesion. In lines 9–11, Casal legitimizes Lucía's expertise in her L1 and takes the opportunity to frame genre learning as situated and additive literacy development. At the time, Casal interpreted Lucía's offer to '*listen more*' and '*talk later about this*' as a learner retreating from a potentially rich interaction. Noting that some students were anxious about the challenge in the early days of the course, he made a joke in line 19 and let the issue rest. It turned out that Lucía preferred to let course activity, and her understanding develop before coming to conclusions, as she returned to it later.

This skepticism became a predictable classroom dynamic; Lucía would express sincere doubt during discussions of many course concepts. In a sense, she regularly held the scientific concepts of class up against her everyday/spontaneous concepts and externalized her observations regarding mismatches, as can be seen regarding word repetition. She also frequently acknowledged that classroom examples were selected to make a point, and so she strongly valued the personal corpus as a means of

Excerpt 6.5 Week two – Class discussion on cohesion

```
1    S1:      repetition +
2    T:       certainly + that's true + repeating words and ideas helps to build cohesion
3             as we discussed in the sample text + you have a question? Lucía?
4    L:       no + not a question
5    T:       that's fine + go on
6    L:       its just that + like + I don't know in English but repetition + it like +
7             does not sound good in Spanish + we do not repeat words that often
8             especially in writing
9    T:       sure + I think it is always fair + and important + to keep in mind that
10            we are not talking about the best way to write + or the only way to write
11            + not in English and not overall + but lets talk about this some more + did
12            you think that there was TOO much repetition in the sample from Swales
13            and Feak? about caffeinated beverages
14   L:       maybe + I mean + like it's a textbook so they probably edited it to make
15            their point (laughs) no + I think its ok + I'll listen to more and we can talk
16            later about this
17   T:       are you sure?
18   L:       yeah yeah
19   T:       hey + I thought you didn't repeat [words (laughs)
20   L:                                        [(laughs)
21   S2:      not in Spanish she said (laughs)
22   class:   (laughter)
```

testing hypotheses. For example, when discussing complex noun phrases, Lucía saw interesting patterns emerge from our text analysis and reflection activities that pointed towards useful ways of making new meanings, but she was not convinced that it was common to create similar structures in her discipline. She stated that '*I just mean that I want to look into my papers in corpus to see,*' while demonstrating a strong awareness of her personal agency in writing decisions: '*I don't think I want to write this way.*' While some of her classmates struggle to develop schematic knowledge of target concepts, to identify them in context, or to verbalize their functional affordances, Lucía is concerned with whether or not she is willing to functionally integrate them into her repertoire.

From assignment to assignment and across drafts of Lucía's final text, her considerable revisions included content-oriented changes and playful experimentation with target concepts. Lucía's submissions were usually characterized by overproduction of target features seen since her last submission, with many uses edited out in subsequent revisions. For example, Lucía's first submission of her final paper had 29 instances of '*this/these + shell noun*' in 21 pages of text, and her final draft had 13. When asked in the text protocol, Lucía explained, '*I like to try, to test these things out. I just want to see how they are useful.*' These 29 instances drew from 16 different shell noun types for diverse topics and functions, and while the structure was overused to the point of distraction in the first draft, it demonstrated a flexible deployment of the construct which was later adjusted in revision. Lucía's explanation reveals the explicit intent to experiment, which resonates with the important affordances of play for testing out and applying developing concepts that were prominent in the work of Vygotsky (Connery *et al.*, 2010).

Before moving to her text protocol and Lucía's reorientation to academic research writing, an important result of Lucía's play is the metalanguage that emerged through her communicative and dialogic languaging in class that mediated her own thinking live but resulted in lasting resources for her classmates. A few examples are a '*checklist*' metaphor to describe inappropriate application of theoretical move frameworks as '*to do lists*,' '*cramming it in*' accompanied by a comical gesture to describe the length of '*Announcing the present research*' sentences in many disciplines, and '*freeze it and front it*' to describe the tendency in engineering sciences to nominalize research processes (freeze) and place them as the focus of sentence, often as the grammatical subject of passive constructions (front). Production of metalanguage demonstrates a movement toward internalization and appropriation in that it provides evidence of decreased reliance on external mediation, conceptual understanding through verbalization, and agency in concept use. Particularly, the checklist metaphor was interesting, in that Lucía introduced it to class to describe an approach she had abandoned. When she successfully adapted the move framework to account for tendencies in her discipline in Week 4, Lucía explained to the class that she '*struggled with the moves*' until she realized that '*the framework is not a to-do checklist.*' She explained that the moves are a '*generalization of the kind of things that people do*' and they can '*help me understand what I'm doing,*' and make locally meaningful decisions, which is precisely the aim.

Moving to the text protocol meeting at the end of the term, Lucía was disappointed in her inability to complete a full draft of her dissertation proposal, in part because of the changes that remote learning had brought to her work habits and workload. In reflecting on her development, she adopts a reader-oriented approach and frames course concepts – particularly shell nouns and rhetorical moves, but also others – as '*options to drive the reader.*' She frames much of the text protocol around interactions with her advisor, which is where Excerpt 6.6 begins. In line 1 Casal revisits a comment Lucía had made regarding her sense of improvement as a writer. Lucía responds as many students in the course have, by indicating that she understands her development through the assessments of her advisor. Lucía expresses her own uncertainty in line 7 ('*maybe it's true*'), and she then describes her advisor's view that her ideas are more organized than they previously were. After many weeks, Lucía returns to the repetition discussion from the early days of class, and in line 19 she reveals that she understood the value of this particular discussion through her advisor's reading of her work. That is, she once more demonstrates a reader-oriented conceptualization of research writing, in that the effects of linguistic and rhetorical decisions are manifest through a reader's interaction with a text.

Importantly, in lines 25 from lines 32 onward, Lucía shares that she has redeployed some of the course concepts as psychological tools for engaging in related, but distinct scholarly activity. That is, Lucía has

Excerpt 6.6 Text protocol Lucía

1	T:	so you said earlier that your writing is im[proving
2	L:	[yeah other people have +
3		other people have [told me yeah
4	T:	[ah (laughs) so other people say so
5	L:	besides you [(laughs)
6	T:	[(laughs) right Lucía + I did just say that
7	L:	(laughs) maybe its true + so like my advisor says so yeah? + and my ideas
8		and text are all over the place in my advisor's words is what he said + and
9		through my way into this class I could not make my head around some +
10		like + some of the techniques like word repetition lexical repetition from
11		the book
12	T:	okay
13	L:	I really did not understand how repeating things would make my text
14		better just as an example of one thing
15	T:	I remember that from the beginning
16	L:	yeah I told you that we don't like do that so much in Spanish and I was
17		really skeptical (frowns in embarrassment)
18	T:	you were + you were very polite though
19	L:	well anyway after some meetings with my advisor I realized that
20		repetitions really made the idea connection much better and he + like he
21		pointed out + some other ways to do it + to connect + and I started
22		applying it myself + when we discuss the SHELL noun idea in class with
23		the packaging idea it got better + and you probably don't remember me
24		being skeptical + because I was like + oh ok + my advisor really liked that
25		when I showed him how I was building connections
26	T:	yeah
27	L:	when I look back now into my original writing + when I look back I can
28		see the ideas that does not match together and incoherent connectors to try
29		and force the connections + now when we talk with my advisor it isn't
30		just that like I can talk about writing when there are problems
31	T:	what do you mean?
32	L:	so like when we are planning a paper he sort of like + walks me through
33		the logic of what I am going to write + and I SURPRISED him by asking
34		what is the gap [(laughs) right
35	T:	[oh (laughs)
36	L:	and what is the territory like why is it important and (says in a deep voice)
37		in recent decades [increasing attention has been paid to (laughs)
38	T:	[(laughs)
39	L:	so I used the moves like to talk about the writing and I think that has been
40		a really like a really obvious way that the class has helped me + its my
41		confidence and my ability to think about and talk about writing with these
42		ideas instead of think about the topic and just talk about it
43	T:	that is really great Lucía + and I think in general you are very good at
44		explaining your thoughts

functionally repurposed the concepts of rhetorical moves (and to a lesser extent shell nouns) to organize discussions of academic writing tasks with her advisor. She indicates that at the onset of a discussion or how to approach a writing task for a collaborative project, rather than take notes on his proposed organization, she prompted him to explain his preferences for how she claims centrality, indicates a gap, and so on, using the rhetorical move concept to frame a planning discussion. This can be taken as strong evidence of flexibly repurposing the conceptual resources of rhetorical moves not to reorient to the genre activity targeted by the course, but to reorganize a separate task. Further, she demonstrates her understanding of form-rhetorical function integration through her joking recitation of a transparent move signal in line 37.

Lucía explicitly states that the impacts of the pedagogical intervention on her has been to her 'ability to think about and talk about writing with these ideas instead of think about the topic and just talk about it,' indicating a metacognitive awareness that the linguistic and rhetorical concepts at the heart of this course are important resources for engaging narrowly in genre-specific writing practices, but can also be abstracted and repurposed for related action.

Conclusions

The two focal students here (Mona and Lucía) show the transformative power of the pedagogy. Aside from evidence that Mona and Lucía moved toward self-regulated use of some target concepts, particularly shell nouns and rhetorical moves, their developmental trajectories mark a transformation to how they think about, talk about, orient to, and engage with the target genre practices in focus. Concept-Based Genre Writing pedagogy has equipped them with new psychological tools for future situated writing activity, but it has also raised their awareness of the situation itself. This includes the community and individual participants of the practice, the purpose for which they engage in the practice, and the importance of making locally meaningful choices. Of course, the individual stories of learners' developmental paths through and out of the course are as diverse as the stories they entered with.

7 Engineering Writing: Context and Pedagogy

Chapters 7 and 8 report a writing tutoring intervention to five L1 Chinese graduate students in Mechanical Engineering, which builds on an earlier corpus- and genre-based intervention conducted at a large public university in North America (see Qiu, 2023). In that study, Qiu (third author) developed a targeted language training module focusing on discipline-appropriate grammatical features at the sentence level. Five students from an engineering writing class volunteered their time to analyze research articles in their field and identify effective discipline-specific communication patterns. As they explored disciplinary texts to map rhetorical functions to linguistic forms, the participants responded positively to the authentic materials and began recognizing the rhetorical purposes behind recurring lexico-grammatical features, such as stance expressions. However, it was also noted during post-intervention interviews that they found learning these linguistic features cognitively demanding and that it was still challenging to apply what they had learned to new contexts (Qiu, 2023). Some participants voluntarily shared difficulties, including one who said that 'It was very much like cramming. I have to absorb large numbers of abstract concepts in a short time span,' and another who expressed 'The stance expressions are the most difficult concept for me to understand. I know I use them, I know they exist, but I cannot connect these dots' (Qiu, 2023: 12–13). The challenge thus lies in ensuring that learners can develop the capacity for self-regulation and independent discovery without becoming overly reliant on guided instruction. Balancing the benefits of direct exposure to language patterns through corpus analysis with the need for meaningful, contextualized communication experiences is essential for fostering a holistic understanding of language use.

To this end, the second intervention study virtually administered in summer 2023, which is presented here in Chapters 7 and 8, pivots to the Concept-Based Genre Writing Pedagogy that taps into the psychological underpinnings of learning abstract concepts and provides grounds for generalization. SCT-informed Concept-Based Language Instruction (C-BLI) was therefore adopted for its high-quality explicit instruction and systematic mediation that engages learners with concepts across a wide range of practical, goal-oriented tasks (Lantolf & Poehner, 2014) in a goal-oriented, genre-based classroom. Methodology-wise, it allows for more direct observation data, such as screen recordings of participants' interaction with the corpus tools and query logs of their input outside of tutoring were needed to unfold concept learning and corpus use in real time.

The Target Concepts

The instructional focus was to teach *clausal subordination* (hereafter, *subordination*), operationalizing effective written communication at the sentence level in Mechanical Engineering (ME) Research Article (RA) writing, as a scientific concept (Haenen et al., 2003; Karpov, 2018; Vygotsky, 1986). It can be oriented to, materialized, verbalized, and internalized by L2 learners as a psychological tool (e.g. Kozulin, 1998; Vygotsky, 1987) that will transform their disciplinary meaning-making processes. This concept was chosen based on a three-pronged needs analysis that draws textual data from discipline-specific sources to demonstrate what sentence-level linguistic knowledge in scientific writing is of concern to engineering students and students in ME in particular: (1) academic writing textbooks for science and engineering fields, (2) instructor feedback on engineering students' scientific writing, and (3) a corpus-based comparative analysis of expert and student writing in ME (see Qiu, 2024a, for a fuller description of the analysis).

Qiu consulted 10 writing textbooks for scientists and engineers based on recommendations from practitioners and graduate students in engineering for an intensive review of common concerns for writing specialists. In a nutshell, the analysis reveals the importance of effective written communication at the sentence level. This concept is not novel; in fact, many engineering writing specialists have covered clausal grammar in their textbooks. All the texts argue for the critical importance of sentence-level clarity and concision in technical writing. For example, Tan (2022) details how sentences can be structured to achieve clarity, vary sentence styles for emphasis and reader engagement, and use conjunctions to connect ideas coherently. The flow of information and the effectiveness of sentence construction are crucial to maintaining reader attention and ensuring clarity. The strategies include, but are not limited to, mixing short and long sentences, varying sentence structure, employing effective transitional phrases, and adding emphasis where needed to produce a 'stream of thought' (Schimel, 2012) that readers can easily track and comprehend. The textbooks also emphasize that authors place important information in strategic locations within a written piece, such as at the start or end of a paragraph. Structural elements such as headings, bullets, and the use of select words as bold or italics are among the tools authors use to draw audience's attention to items they consider critical. Notwithstanding these important guidelines, language-focused instruction in engineering writing often distills them into a set of rules that, though well-intentioned, may not readily translate into a coherent concept to orient performance.

For the needs analysis of instructor feedback, Qiu consulted the instructor of an existing Academic Engineering Writing course who has been collecting previous student deliverables for her own research agenda. She consented Qiu's participation in her study and shared her repository of student writing, including first and final drafts with her feedback. The data set consisted of 769 distinct comments drawn from 30 individual student drafts. Broadly speaking, the instructor feedback can be construed as feedback on local-level writing skills (Diction, Format, Mechanics) and global-level writing skills (Citation, Fluidity, Organization, Rhetorical Expectation, Sentence Effectiveness, Stance). It was found that the instructor feedback focused less on local-level skills such as Mechanics and Format (less than 10% in total) but more heavily on global-level skills like effective communication at sentence level, idea development, literature synthesis, information flow and part-genre-specific expectation. This ostensible imbalance evinces that the instructor in her pedagogy foregrounded the development of ideas, synthesis of literature, concise sentence structure and appropriate stance construction.

The needs analysis of the corpus-based comparison between expert and student writing aimed to provide a linguistic-descriptive analysis of ME research writing in published RAs and manuscripts of advanced student RA writing. Qiu retrieved sentence-level linguistic features by systematically identifying simple, compound, and complex sentences in the texts. The analysis focused on *subordination*, which plays an integral role in complex sentence formation – a dominant sentence type in the ME expert writing (see also Conrad, 2017). To examine how students' use of subordination differed from that of experts, he then profiled the distribution of syntactic as well as discourse-functional subtypes of *subordination* between the two writer groups. It was discovered that some structural and functional categories of subordination were used significantly less by student writers in ME. This finding resulted in a detailed textual analysis of sentences within these categories to render some common linguistic themes. Integrating this insight with the results from the other two needs analyses, Qiu arrived at four sentence-level linguistic concepts: Types of Clauses, Intra-Sentence Discoursal Functions, Grammatical Stance Expressions, and Inter-Sentence Flow and Emphasis. That is, to meaningfully incorporate the linguistic concept of subordination into ME RA writing, the concept of *subordination* was broken down into four discipline-appropriate sub-concepts.

Type of Clauses

A sentence structure can be simple, compound, or complex. A simple sentence contains only one independent clause, which can have one or more subjects but only one predicate. A compound sentence has two coordinated (e.g. *and*, *or*, *but*, *so*) independent clauses. A complex sentence has one independent clause plus at least one dependent clause, which cannot stand alone. The finiteness of a clause is determined by the tense of the main predicate. If the main verb is tense-inflected (e.g. *walked*, *did*), it is a finite verb. This concept is considered the foundational concept for the following three concepts because students will miss the opportunity to develop functional control of their writing without a systematic understanding of the form. Although students at doctoral level had at least a decade of English education and so all come with a good grasp of basic English grammar, they nevertheless require some explicit instruction to activate that part of knowledge in their mind and check if their prior education aligns with this one in terms of, for example, the definition of clause.

Intra-Sentence Discoursal Functions

Two ideas can be effectively connected in a single, complex sentence when each idea is relatively simple and the relationship between the ideas is important. The intra-sentence structure is more complex than in a simple sentence, but the sentence must still be concise, precise, and easy to read. By comparing a corpus of student-produced RA manuscripts to that of published RA writing in ME, subordinate structures that realize different discoursal functions in a text were statistically compared. The discourse-functional taxonomization adopted here follows the functional analysis of formulaic sequences by Simpson-Vlach and Ellis (2010). Those which diverged from expert use in the published RA writing were deemed 'challenging' for novice disciplinary writers; whereas those which aligned with expert use were deemed 'common' discoursal functions in ME RA writing. Challenging functions include intertextual reference (which identifies previous findings or known information), intratextual reference (which orients readers to textual, tabular or graphic data), evaluation (which expresses evaluative viewpoints of information) and directives (which instructs readers to perform an action or to see things in a way determined by the writer). Common functions include semantic relationships of time, manner, purpose, condition, result and concession.

Grammatical Stance Expressions

The expression of stance, defined broadly as expressions of attitudes, epistemic judgments, and interpersonal involvement, is increasingly recognized as an important feature of both expert and student academic writing. It is the way that writers intrude to stamp their personal feelings and assessments (including attitudes that a speaker has about certain information, how certain they are about its credibility, how they obtained access to the information, and what perspective they are taking) onto their arguments or step back and disguise their involvement. It is bound by disciplinary conventions and can be revealed through different lexical or grammatical choices such as the use of first-person pronouns. Grammatical stance devices include two distinct linguistic components, one presenting the stance and the other presenting a proposition that is framed by that stance. Stance expressed at the sentence level mostly takes the form of complement clauses. Building on the Intra-Sentence Discoursal Functions, this concept brings more structural variations within stance complement clauses from expert and student writing based on Biber *et al.*'s (1999) profiling of grammatical stance devices and Hyland's (2005) interactional metadiscourse framework to highlight the importance of exercising discipline-appropriate authorial voice and writerly intent regarding making claims in an academic text.

Inter-Sentence Flow and Emphasis

In English written communication, one of the most important ways to facilitate readers' understanding is to initiate a clause with given or background information and ends with new information, known as old-new information flow (see Halliday & Hasan, 1976, for further discussion of information structure), so that readers could progress smoothly from the preceding sentence to the next without the risk of being 'thrown off the cliff.' Known information is (1) an item was previously introduced in the text, (2) an 'anchor' of known information is in a phrase with new information, (3) an item is known from the context of the situation, (4) an item is easily inferable from previous statements, and (5) an item is part of shared background information that is easily available in readers' minds. New information is (1) completely new ideas, (2) ideas that were mentioned so long ago in the text that readers won't have them in mind, and (3) ideas that are part of the readers' world knowledge but are so unrelated to the topic that readers won't have them readily accessible. There are four effective ways to maintain a good intersentence information flow: (1) repetition or nominalization, (2) a dependent clause + independent clause sequence, (3) extraposed *it* complement clause, and (4) *this/these* + signaling nouns construction. In addition to the flow, a good cohesive text has a proper emphasis on the right material. Emphasis is essential to clarity as it stresses the primary ideas of sentences and paragraphs. There are three effective ways to maintain a proper emphasis: (1) emphasis by position, (2) emphasis by sentence length, and (3) emphasis by repetition.

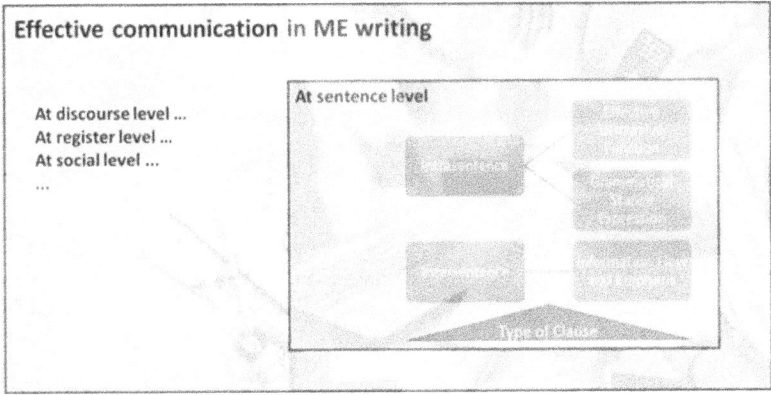

Figure 7.1 Visual conceptualization of sentence-level linguistic knowledge

As depicted in Figure 7.1, the four key sub-concepts represent different layers involved in understanding effective communication in Mechanical Engineering writing, specifically at the sentence level. Type of Clause provides the foundation, referring to underlying grammatical knowledge about clauses that is a prerequisite for properly matching clausal forms with rhetorical functions. Effective Discoursal Functions and Grammatical Stance Expressions are categorized under intra-sentence features, since both relate to how clauses operate within a sentence. Information Flow and Emphasis fall under inter-sentence relationships – examining how ideas flow and connect across sentence boundaries.

Pedagogical Materials Development

Now that we have chosen the concepts, how do we visualize them meaningfully for participants to be mediated during instruction instead of teaching the abstract concepts mechanically? Since C-BLI is predicated on particular ways of accounting for, presenting, and internalizing material (cf. Chapter 2), visual charts and 'learning tools' must be carefully designed. Learners explicitly learn these tools, which are considered necessary resources for internalizing concepts and facilitating development. The goal is not to teach linguistic forms as mechanical features, but rather to build conceptual understandings that capture the function-form relationship underlying language use in context so that learners can make local-level decisions agentively based on principles. The psychological affordance of conceptual models as meditational devices rests on their ability to direct learners in the executive component of communicative activities and induce L2 development.

Given the value of materialized concepts as visual models, the next question is, what kind of visualization attunes to Mechanical Engineering students? In the textual, diagrammatic, and symbolic representational systems used in Mechanical Engineering education, numerous visualizations exist, including diagrams, flowcharts, and graphs. While diagrams are the predominant visual representation (Gieskes *et al.*, 2012) extensively used in foundational Mechanical Engineering courses (e.g. free-body diagrams), flowcharts have proven useful for mediating problem-based learning (Gencer, 2023), a critical skill specified in the Accreditation Board for Engineering and Technology (ABET). Flowcharts employ visual elements – boxes and arrows – to systematically map procedural sequences from initiation to completion. In this instructional context, the flowchart breaks down sentence-level linguistic concepts into a series of decision-making pathways through both form-focused and meaning-focused questions (Swaroop *et al.*, 2023). Their utility for systematically describing approaches makes them ideally suited as graphical representations of discrete process steps (Heiser & Schikora, 2001). These questions guide students through deliberate choices, such as selecting appropriate clause types based on their communicative intentions. This systematic, process-oriented approach aligns with a fundamental principle of C-BLI – providing learners with explicit material mediation that 'gives the conceptual properties of the action a material form' (Johnson, 2008: 73). Students can leverage this pedagogical tool until decision-making sequentiality becomes internalized.

While flowcharts have proven effective as didactic models in C-BLI approaches to teaching grammar (Negueruela, 2003), sarcasm (Kim, 2013), and authorial voice (Fogal, 2015), flowcharts in general could be misinterpreted as similar to traditional prescriptive rules in L2 instruction if not properly implemented. At first glance, the decision boxes in a flowchart might seem to function similarly to prescriptive rules. However, the distinction lies in how flowcharts fundamentally transform the learning process: they enable learners to actively weigh contextual factors (e.g. '*can it stand alone as a complete sentence*' in Figure 7.4) rather than applying uniform rules divorced from context. When students use the Type of Clause flowchart, for example, their engagement with the decision-making process – regardless of whether they reach the conventionally 'correct' answer – demonstrates their agency in navigating the chart and develops crucial metalinguistic awareness. This approach provides learners with a psychological tool to articulate their reasoning by tracing their path through the decision boxes, allowing them to pinpoint exactly where their interpretation diverges from others. Such procedural knowledge (Karpov, 2003), previously unavailable to learners, is meaningful and transferrable; it transforms potential 'errors' into opportunities for metalinguistic discussion and deeper conceptual understanding.

In the present study, Qiu developed the first version of the Type of Clause flowchart (Figure 7.2) by referencing previous scholarship on flowcharting grammatical concepts and scholarly interpretations of the

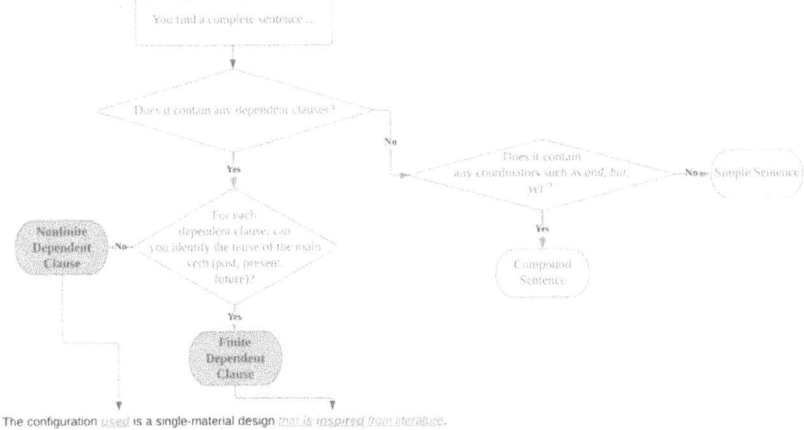

Figure 7.2 The first version of the flowchart for Type of Clause

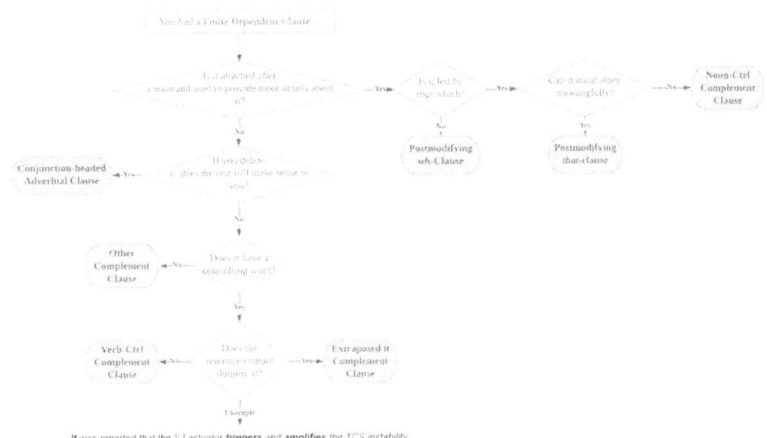

Figure 7.3 The first version of the flowchart for type of finite clause

four grammatical concepts (e.g. Biber *et al.*, 1999; Fogal, 2015; Negueruela, 2003). It features one starting node, three decision diamonds, four terminal nodes, an example sentence, and aims to model the thought process for identifying English clause types. To follow it, students first need to understand what constitutes a dependent clause and verb tense. The next challenge is classifying finite and nonfinite dependent clauses into structural subtypes (see Figure 7.3), which is more difficult than distinguishing a dependent versus coordinate clause. As shown, the first decision differentiates noun-modifying clauses, which are structurally determined to follow a noun/phrase, from less structurally bound clauses. For noun-modifying clauses, a key difference (the structural and semantic completeness of the clause) exists between post-modifying (relative) and noun complement clauses. The remaining decisions separate complement clauses from adverbials, then subdivide complement clauses into Extraposed *it*, Verb-controlled, and Other complement clauses. Most decisions rely on form-based cues and are thus straightforward. Two meaning-based decisions require agentive 'sense-making': '*If you move it to the beginning of the sentence, does the rest still make sense?*' and '*Can it stand alone as a complete sentence?*' Both will accompany explicit instruction during the tutoring.

After a discussion with a V-SCT colleague, Qiu made several modifications to improve comprehension guidance (see Figure 7.4), including rewording the two potentially ambiguous meaning-based decisions for clarity. Qiu also incorporated colleagues' suggestions to define 'controlling word' in the chart, avoiding cross-referencing materials. The revised version underwent piloting with non-participant engineering students and yielded suggestions for further refinement. Qiu repeated this process (Figure 7.5) for each concept's flowchart.

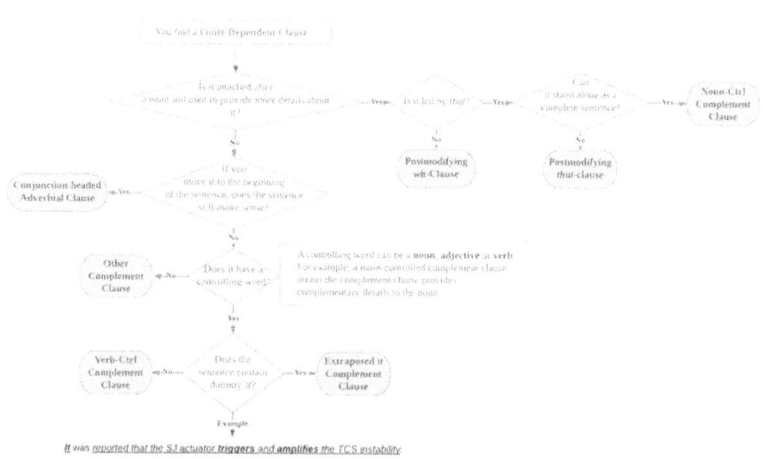

Figure 7.4 The final version of the flowchart for type of finite clause

Figure 7.5 The process of flowchart development

Description of Pedagogy and Data Sources

After determining which flowcharts to use, each linguistic sub-concept was integrated into the intervention sequence, as depicted within the 'Tutoring Intervention (Remote)' box in Figure 7.6. C-BLI places emphasis on a learner's agency to develop their cognition with the teacher playing as a mediator (Johnson, 2009). As reviewed in Chapter 2, C-BLI concretizes the learning process in six phases: pre-understanding, concept presentation, materialization, verbalization/languaging, performance and internalization (see Poehner & Lantolf, 2024: 19). The procedure was adapted to disciplinary research writing instruction with flexibility. That is, students did not follow one step after the other in a linear order. Rather, most phases were present in each course activity. L2 learners have at their disposal an Orienting Basis for Action (OBA) based on their previous learning experiences. The objective is to internalize a Scheme of Complete Orienting Basis of Action (SCOBA), which is an externally presented scheme for the completion of an action. Rather than replacing learners' existing OBA with the instructor's scientific presentation, the goal is to help them develop a new, more comprehensive basis for action that incorporates both their prior knowledge and the scientific concepts being taught.

In this spirit, the four sub-concepts identified above are featured in an instructional unit in the tutoring. The activity sequence of each instructional unit began with a teacher-led presentation of an abstract linguistic concept (30 mins), followed by a teacher-mediated Sentence Rewriting activity (30 mins) and a step-by-step Corpus Query activity (30 mins), and ended with a student-centered Self-Assessment of the taught concept in

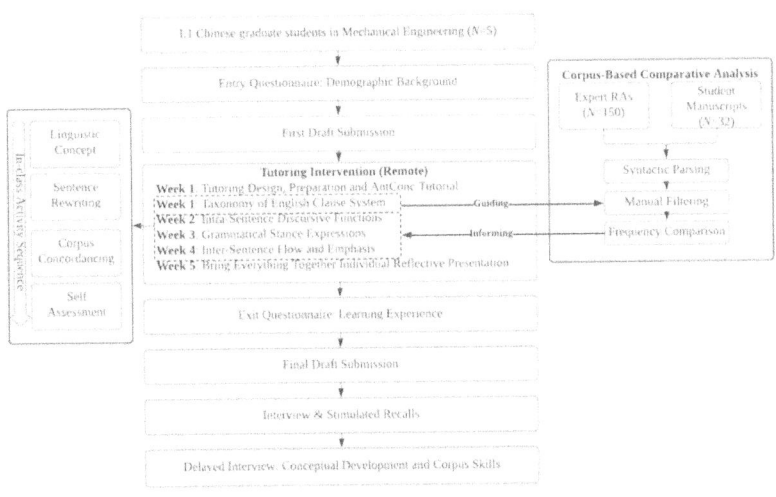

Figure 7.6 The tutoring design

their own draft (30 mins). The SCOBAs, in the form of flowcharts, were available and used for material mediation by the participants throughout the tutoring if/as needed. After the end of the instruction, participants appropriated the concepts to make new decisions in revising their RA manuscripts. Together with an introductory session and a summary session of students' reflective presentations, this tutoring featured six 120-min lessons to help advanced L2 student writers improve their writing and revising skills for publication purposes in Mechanical Engineering. The introductory session also featured a one-hour AntConc tutorial for students to download the software and class corpus, and practice some concordancing functionalities with guidance, including sorting, advanced search, wildcards, collocation, and wordlist.

Also shown in Figure 7.6 are the various data sources collected at different time points during the study. Data is prepared with two primary goals: (1) to provide insights into the quality of the learner experiences engaged in this pedagogical activity; (2) to assess the impacts of the novel pedagogy on L2 graduate-level genre-based writing through a genetic conceptualization of development (Lantolf & Thorne, 2006). For understanding the learner experiences in the tutoring intervention, Qiu collected learner perception data including entry and exit questionnaires (administered immediately before and after the intervention, respectively), initial and final drafts of a for-publication RA manuscript, reflective presentation materials (administered in Week 5), and semi-structured post-intervention and delayed interviews. For the study of conceptual development as an outcome of the tutoring intervention, Qiu collected three types of data: definition data, discourse data, and verbalization data, in line with previous assessments of C-BLI (in particular, Negueruela, 2003). In Chapter 8, Qiu will concentrate on the verbalization data, building on the broader methodological framework detailed in Qiu's unpublished doctoral dissertation (Qiu, 2024b).

Participants

The five participants, recruited from the Department of Mechanical Engineering at two engineering-intensive universities in China, received virtual tutoring instruction. In terms of participants' overall English proficiency level, they all reported their scores in the College English Test Band 6 (CET-6). In China, the CET carries substantial weight in university education and beyond. It serves not only as a crucial academic requirement for non-English major university students but often as a prerequisite for job applications, graduate school admission, and professional advancement. Many employers list CET certification as a basic requirement, and universities commonly integrate CET scores into their graduation criteria. According to an alignment study by Jin *et al.* (2022), these participants' English proficiency levels corresponded to B1-B2 on the Common European Framework of Reference for Languages (CEFR). Qiu obtained informed consent and compensated participants for their time in the study. Table 7.1 displays the tutee profiles.

Participants all came with unique sub-disciplinary backgrounds which intersect with disciplines such as Computer Science, Material Science, and Chemistry. This may have had an impact on their writing and publishing expectations, but they expressed familiarity with some ME journals that the author selected for the corpus-based comparative analysis and felt motivated to work with such data. As for the target genre, all indicated the pressing need to publish internationally in peer-reviewed journals during graduate studies and had crafted an RA-like draft ready for revision before the start of the intervention.

Two of the five participants reported that they had at least one first-author English publication. And three of them had some prior academic writing instruction experience, but none had participated in any corpus workshop before. In reflecting on their strengths and weaknesses

Table 7.1 Overview of tutoring participants

Participants	Pengfei	Lincai	Geyao	Jiuyue	Jiangke
Gender, Age	M, 25	M, 25	F, 24	F, 29	M, 24
English Learning	16 years	11 years	18 years	16 years	10 years
Level of Study	1st PhD	1st PhD	1st PhD	3rd PhD	2nd Master's
Subfield	Micro-nano manufacturing	Composite structure	Bio-manufacturing	Material processing	Artificial intelligence
Publication?	N	N	N	Y	Y
Academic Writing Instruction?	Y	N	Y	Y	N
Corpus use?	N	N	N	N	N
English Level	CET-6: 430	CET-6: 450	CET-6: 579	CET-6: 497	CET-4: 489
Computer Skills	COMSOL, Vision, Origin	Matlab, Python, Abaqus	Visio, 3DS Max, Origin	PS, Origin	Python, Matlab, draw.io
Strength	Grammar	Grammar	Grammar	Experience in writing	I enjoy writing; Use of Chinese
Weakness	Advanced sentence pattern; Use of Chinese	Vocabulary and sentence structure	Coherence, logic	Grammar; Uses of Chinese	Vocabulary is limited
Writing Resources	YouDao, Zhiyun & CNKI translation	DeepL translation, ChatGPT	DeepL translation, ChatGPT	Grammarly	DeepL & Baidu translation

Note. Names are all pseudonyms chosen by tutees themselves. Both strength and weakness are self-reports from the entry questionnaire.

in writing for academic purposes, the five participants showed several notable patterns in their technical backgrounds and English writing experiences. Multiple participants demonstrated programming proficiency, with both Lincai and Jiangke skilled in Python and MATLAB. Origin software, a data analysis and graphing tool, was an expertise shared among the other three. In terms of language abilities in English writing, grammar emerged as a common strength for two participants, though interestingly, it remained a challenge for Jiuyue. The reliance on their L1 Chinese in English composing was a shared concern, specifically noted by Pengfei and Jiuyue. Regarding writing support tools, DeepL translation platform was the most commonly used resource. ChatGPT 3.5 was also utilized by multiple participants as a writing aid.

Data Source

As one of the conditions for developing mental actions in Gal'perin's approach as a tool for internalizing features, verbalization activities include students (1) explaining in writing to the instructor the rationale for applying a particular concept to solving a linguistic problem in their first draft during Self-Assessment activities and (2) explaining orally to the instructor the rationale for choosing a particular materialized object (e.g. flowcharts, the concordancing tool) to solve a linguistic problem in their first draft during post-intervention revisions. These explanations were provided in the students' first language (Chinese), although occasionally a few of them freely opted for English. Aligning with SCT's commitment to genetic analysis, this chapter makes a methodological contribution by simultaneously tracking two genetic domains of concept development. The microgenetic domain is captured through real-time documentation of learners' interactions with materials (i.e. the 'performance' phase), making visible the moment-to-moment unfolding of understanding. The ontogenetic domain is accessed through retrospective reflections. Qiu looked at how these immediate interactions connect to learners' broader developmental trajectory through various verbalization opportunities. This approach provides a coherent picture of concept formation than traditional single-time-scale analyses.

Definition activity handouts

This definition activity was administered three times during the study. At the beginning of each instructional unit, students were asked to define the linguistic concept that they were going to learn in that session. At the end, students completed the same definition activity as part of the Self-Assessment activities (serving as the last question) after the completion of all activities. At delayed interviews, this last time students were asked again the same questions to explain the meaning behind the use of the linguistic concepts that have been covered in class to assess the sustainability of their conceptual understanding. Definition data collected were in English, but students were recorded using online translations to help convert their L1 understanding of the concept into L2 since they were all intermediate-level English learners. An example definition activity is given in Chapter 8, and the rest can be found in Qiu (2024b).

Sentence rewriting activity handouts

Students received complex example sentences from expert or student writing in ME. Their task is to use the flowcharts as psychological tools for thinking to identify specific linguistic features based on learned concepts. This includes labeling clauses with taxonomic categories and functions. In this manner, learners can employ the didactic models to verbally explicate the meaning of appropriate disciplinary linguistic concepts to themselves. These discourse activities promote intentional use of the linguistic concept and heightened attention to the strong form-function mappings within sentences from their field.

Corpus query activity handouts

During tutoring of each linguistic concept, students were asked to complete a Corpus Query Activity online, guided by step-by-step instructions. The purpose was to familiarize participants with the concordancing experience via AntConc and have them practice complex query syntax using wildcards (e.g. '*', '[]') and part of speech tags (e.g. '_VBG', '_JJ'). Each activity was designed based on the comparative analysis of expert and student writing in ME, where in Inter-Sentence Flow and Emphasis, experts were found to use unattended *this* much more frequently as a cohesive device than that of students.

Self-assessment activity handouts

Students selected two to three paragraphs from their own drafts and informally identify and annotate the linguistic concept learned in class, using visual cues such as highlighting or arrows. Next, focusing deeply on a few sentences, students evaluated linguistic choices made by asking themselves why sentences take their existing forms. This meta-cognitive step encourages them to verbalize their understanding to someone else of the focal concepts and how they made decisions about using the concepts in their writing. Meanwhile, it develops awareness of potential function-form mapping. Ultimately, the analysis developed skills in diagnosing trouble spots and devising conceptually sound planning for subsequent revisions.

Screen recordings

Videotaping subjects as they compose provides an alternative to think-aloud protocols for a real-time record of the cognitive composing process. Students were asked to record their screen by the freeware OBS Studio during in-class activities (Sentence Rewriting, Corpus Query, Self-Assessment) and post-intervention revision and upload the recordings one at a time onto a private digital folder (shared only with Qiu) via MS OneDrive. Of particular concern with L2 students is that many writers may generate ideas in their native language as they compose (Cumming, 1989). Furthermore, it allows the researcher to interrogate process-enriched episodes, where students encountered cognitive dissonance in internalizing the conceptual knowledge through material mediation.

Stimulated recalls

The stimulated recalls, conducted within a week of final draft submission, served both as a research method to understand participants' revision processes and as an additional pedagogical space for conceptual development (Johnson & Golombek, 2016). During each recall session conducted via Zoom, both the participant and the author could pause the revision recording to discuss specific revisions. This shared control over the discussion fostered collaborative dialogue about participants' purposes, strategies, and resource use. While Qiu had prepared participant-tailored questions about noteworthy episodes in advance, the sessions were intentionally structured to allow participants to initiate discussion of revisions they found significant. These sessions thus created opportunities for participants to verbalize their understanding of concepts and for responsive mediation of that understanding. To maintain a moderate level of engagement in this mediational dialogue during longer revision recordings, we took regular breaks and fast-forwarded through segments where neither had substantive comments.

Analytical Procedures

The data analysis procedures for investigating L2 development as a conceptual process emerge from the SCT understanding of communication and development. Communication is defined as an activity through which social meanings are appropriated, self-awareness in expression develops, mutual understanding and influence occur, action and activities are self-regulated, and new meanings emerge through the transcendence of socially established norms (Marková, 1979: 45). Language development is re-conceptualized as a revolutionary process where conceptual meanings change and evolve at the same time that their relationship to specific language features is also reshaped (Negueruela, 2003). L2 development is about the conscious appropriation, internalization, mastery, and transgression of L2 meanings (grammatical or otherwise) that can orient L2 learners in communicative activity.

Qiu analyzed students' verbalization data where (1) they were asked to define each linguistic concept at three timepoints (before, immediately after, and two months after the tutoring), (2) they performed sequentially in-class Sentence Rewriting, Corpus Query and Self-Assessment Activities to make their understanding of the concept comprehensible to the instructor, and (3) they explained their linguistic choices in revising sentences from their own draft during a stimulated recall session to trace the coherence of their reasoning using the presented theoretical concepts as cognitive tools. This Vygotskian approach examines concepts in formation as tools for problem-solving. The learning tool of verbalization aids internalization while providing data on students' evolving conceptualization. Learners recorded self-explanations in three formats: (1) in written form during the definition task before, immediately after, and two months after the tutoring, (2) in written form in Sentence Rewriting, Corpus Query, and Self-Assessment activities, and (3) in oral form in stimulated recalls regarding their draft revisions. This allows observation of theoretical concepts they actively deployed. Explanations vary in quality, from rote memorization to systematic reasoning. Unlike retrospective reports, self-explanations involve concurrent conceptual deployment. More importantly, these verbalizations reveal emerging conceptual orientations.

Analysis of definition data followed a heuristic that Qiu developed in his dissertation. This framework was developed by Bruner *et al.* (1956) and first introduced to classroom teaching of scientific concepts in Joyce *et al.* (1997). In history teacher education, Haenen *et al.*'s (2003) distinctions clarify five integral elements in instruction on academic concepts in order to expand the framework toward greater pedagogical utility for the teaching and development of conceptual knowledge: (1) designating a name for the concept, (2) positive and negative examples of concept application, (3) the essential features for subsuming cases within the concept, (4) acceptable variation in how essential features may present, and (5) a working definition summarizing the concept rule. An example definition of Grammatical Stance Expression is provided in Table 7.2, which conveys attitudinal, epistemic or affective standpoint in utterances through grammatical choices. Qiu examined students' definitions of key concepts made at three points: (1) before instruction, (2) immediately after the corresponding instructional unit, and (3) in delayed interviews. From a sociocultural perspective, attaining awareness and control of theoretical concepts serves as a driving force in advancing L2 development. Instruction that fosters this process is developmental. The notion of linguistic awareness here refers to students' ability to explicate concepts to others, representing a form of explanatory performance. In sum, the heuristic allows for systematic evaluation of the key qualities represented

Table 7.2 A definition of grammatical stance expressions

Name of the concept	Grammatical stance expression	
	Positive	Negative
Examples	Some studies <u>suggest that cancer cells may experience frequent and transitory nuclear envelope ruptures</u>. (hedging)	The equations we employ here <u>are from standard models available in duly mentioned references</u>.
Attributes	Position; Evaluation; Self-mention	Propositional
Values	Occur at word, phrase and clause level; Signs of making discipline-appropriate claims	Objective delivery of factual information
Rule	The expression of stance is defined broadly as expression of attitudes, epistemic judgments, and interpersonal involvement. Grammatical stance devices include two distinct linguistic components, one presenting the stance and the other presenting a proposition that is framed by that stance.	

in learners' definitions of theoretical concepts, providing insight into their potential to support sustained conceptual development.

Analysis of the participants' materialized action drew on students' recording of their task performance in Sentence Rewriting and Corpus Query activities during instruction. By tracking their ongoing usage of target forms through interaction with different materials, Qiu can investigate conceptual development of discipline-appropriate linguistic knowledge in its functional, 'executive' domain where students notice and correct their prior incomplete understanding of it. Again, based on a heuristic developed in his unpublished dissertation (Qiu, 2024b), Qiu analyzed student performance for (1) their procedural coherence in engaging with course materials, AntConc, and online translation tools, (2) their execution patterns in applying the linguistic concepts (ranging from systematic to haphazard approaches), and (3) evidence of learning outcomes through both successful and labored interactions with materials during writing tasks.

Analysis of Self-Assessment activity handouts entailed a qualitative approach (Richards, 2003) to analyze students' performance and written explanations of key concepts. All learner-written texts invoking the linguistic concepts at these time points were analyzed on these parameters to trace their explanatory value for internalization. By close reading of the handouts, Qiu identified student responses for (1) their ability to correctly identify the concept in sample sentences from their writing, (2) their explanation in applying these concepts (with or without material mediation) to their writing, and (3) evidence of deepened understanding through the act of explanation itself. The final analysis focused on mapping patterns in how students articulated their understanding and tracing how the process of explaining concepts to others potentially enhanced their own comprehension. Qiu learned firsthand how each participant was able to appropriate the linguistic concept they had just learned to their own writing task.

The analysis of oral data from post-intervention stimulated recalls began with transcription using Kultura, followed by manual editing on its interface. The resultant texts were segmented into idea units and subjected to content analysis in Atlas.ti. To ensure reliability, Qiu developed initial coding that was used to train a colleague in coding. This process yielded four broad categories: conceptual awareness, learning and evaluation, problem-solving, and revising strategies. For the present purposes, rather than presenting aggregate results of participants' revision processes, Qiu selected representative moments when participants verbalized their rationale for real-time decisions during revision, which may provide growth points for development, particularly focusing on their agentive use of different materials and problem-solving strategies.

The data analysis procedures aligned with both SCT's understanding of L2 development as conscious meaning-making and genre theory's emphasis on writers' developing rhetorical awareness and repertoire in discourse communities. To examine this developmental process, this context chapter has summarized the analysis of learners' verbalizations – captured in visual, oral, and written forms – to provide insights into how students appropriated genre conventions and explained their linguistic choices. In the analysis chapter that follows, Qiu will trace how a focal learner (Geyao) deployed theoretical concepts in her performance and verbalization data. A close examination of the participant's explanation of the concepts during the definition task, the Sentence Rewriting, Corpus Query, and Self-Assessment activities, and the post-intervention revision process will hopefully assess her emerging conceptual orientations and the process of internalization.

8 Engineering Writing: Findings and Implications

This chapter analyzes the conceptual development trajectory of a focal student (Geyao) in understanding and applying Grammatical Stance Expressions through Concept-Based Genre Writing pedagogy. The analysis traces her journey across multiple timepoints and activities, examining how her understanding evolved from pre-understanding phase through materialization and performance tasks and ultimately to verbalization and internalization. Drawing on Vygotsky's (1986) recognition that the teaching–learning context offers an ideal environment for studying conceptual development, this chapter documents Geyao's learning progression through analysis of her verbal protocols, material interactions, and recorded writing revision process.

The chapter is structured chronologically to reconstruct key developmental phases. It begins by examining Geyao's prior knowledge and initial conceptualization of Grammatical Stance Expressions, providing important context about her academic background and writing needs. The analysis then moves through her engagement with materialization activities, including Sentence Rewriting and Corpus Query tasks, where she began applying the scientific concepts with guidance. Her subsequent performance in Self-Assessment activities reveals how she started to use the concepts to analyze her own writing. The chapter examines her revised definition immediately after instruction, followed by a detailed analysis of her post-intervention revision process through screen recordings and stimulated recall sessions. Finally, it analyzes her delayed definition two months after the intervention to assess sustained development.

At each stage, the analysis focuses on both her explicit verbalizations and her interactions with pedagogical materials and tools. Performance in activities is evaluated through frequency and quality of material engagement, while revision processes are analyzed with an eye toward problem-solving patterns. This multi-perspective analysis reveals key insights about the role of metalinguistic awareness, strategic use of digital and pedagogical resources, and the importance of conceptual learning processes in developing academic writing competence for advanced ESL/EFL learners in engineering disciplines.

Geyao's Development of Grammatical Stance Expressions

Geyao's prior knowledge of the sentence-level linguistic concepts in engineering writing

Geyao was a first-year PhD student in the department of mechanical engineering. Like other participants in the study, she came from a unique sub-disciplinary background that intersects with biomanufacturing. As an EFL student working and studying in an EFL educational context, she had been learning English for 18 years at the time of the study, despite the fact that her exposure had been very limited to English for testing or publication purposes. Admittedly, her experience thinking and writing in English has been temporary and unnatural. In terms of her prior English writing training, Geyao received academic writing instruction during her undergraduate and post-graduate studies, but she spoke extensively in the end-of-term interview about how they were different from this intervention. In particular, the focus of her undergraduate English academic writing course was on a generic understanding of the organizational structure. Moving up to the graduate level, the emphasis shifted to interdisciplinary communication and presentation skills. It is reasonable to hypothesize that she had not developed a coherent understanding of sentence-level linguistic knowledge. That is to say, like many EFL learners, she had not been previously mediated to the orienting potential of the English language to understand the rhetorical writing expectations commonly upheld in scholarly/academic research publications in engineering prior to this intervention. Her later encounter with the linguistic approach to writing instruction exposed significant challenges in meeting disciplinary writing demands – challenges that her previous training had not prepared her to address.

During her study, Geyao faced a constant challenge among Chinese academics – the pressure to publish in English-medium peer-reviewed journals. Despite her extensive 18-year journey with English learning and a commendable CET-6 score of 579 that placed her among the more proficient English users in the study cohort, she found herself at a crossroads typical of many emerging scholars in China's STEM fields. While she had mastered the formal aspects of English grammar and the technical knowledge of the subject matter, she struggled with the more tacit aspects of academic writing – specifically, creating effective arguments and maintaining a coherent and logical flow in reporting her work. Like many of her generation, Geyao embraced technological solutions to bridge these gaps. She turned to modern writing aids, particularly DeepL translation and the recently released ChatGPT 3.5, to help her navigate the complexities of academic English. These tools became her digital tutor as she worked to transform her ideas into publishable research. The stakes were high for Geyao. Recognizing the need for additional support beyond digital tools, she had already taken proactive steps toward her publication goals. When an opportunity arose through her English for Academic Purposes instructor for discipline-specific writing tutoring in which Qiu was seeking participants, she reached out instantly and volunteered to participate. Weeks before the time the tutoring began, she had carefully crafted a research article draft that awaited revision.

Before each instructional unit was presented, Geyao was asked to provide a formal definition of the new linguistic concept in the class handout. Of the four linguistic concepts, Grammatical Stance Expressions is considered the most conceptually challenging area for the study participants to comprehend and use appropriately. Two participants lacked evidence of deepened understanding or application of the stance form-function mapping intended by the tutoring. Their difficulties in moving beyond initial conceptualizations to embrace the more systematic aspects of the learning unit indicate the challenges inherent in achieving a comprehensive, functional grasp of this linguistic concept. Therefore, in what follows, Qiu compares Geyao's response to this concept at this timepoint with the scientific presentation of this concept. In addition to her textual output, supplementary analysis is drawn from post-intervention semi-structured interviews of her retrospective thoughts, including whether they have consulted sources to finish these assignments and why.

Grammatical Stance Expressions convey attitudinal, epistemic, or affective standpoints in utterances through grammatical choices. It is this capacity to qualify and present calculated points of view that distinguishes more rhetorically sophisticated writing from writing that presents information with minimal explicit stance-taking. In the instructional unit, Qiu introduced the flowchart (Figure 8.1) and included the means by which speakers can hedge or boost their commitment to the epistemic certainty of what they say (*Do you want to express a certain position?*). Modal verbs, evidential adjuncts, approximative adverbs, reporting clauses, conditionals, or probability descriptors are the primary resources

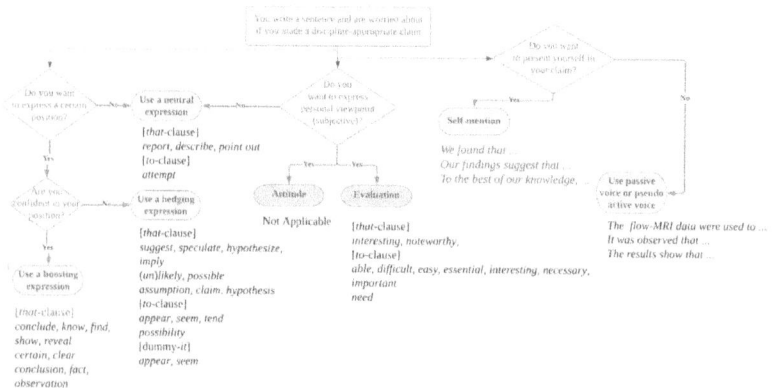

Figure 8.1 A flowchart of grammatical stance expressions

employed in the ME corpus data. Typically, stance marking couples an explicit evaluation component with a propositional content segment, such as framing (*Do you want to express personal viewpoint?*). For instance, in Example 8.1 from the class corpus, the adjective-controlled complement clause ('*possible to reduce . . .*') functions as an epistemic hedging device toward the factual outcome claim. This linguistic framing allows writers to appropriately qualify and modulate the reliability of their assertions based on disciplinary conventions. Stance devices are also used to mark personal involvement in a research activity (*Do you want to present yourself in your claim?*) through self-mentions or disguise it through passivized constructions or pseudo-active constructions. Stance resources thereby serve both interpersonal risk-mitigation and metadiscoursal functions within ME research writing.

Example 8.1: With the stage model, **it is possible to reduce** the computation time by applying periodic conditions in the rotating direction. (ME corpus)

As seen in Table 8.1, Geyao demonstrated an initial understanding of stance expressions that, while partially accurate, revealed significant room for development. Her pre-tutoring definition captured one fundamental component – the expression of attitude and evaluation – and correctly identified an important function of stance – establishing authorial control over research findings. During the post-intervention interview, she clarified that her reference to 'specific words' primarily meant evaluative adjectives, which are but one linguistic resource available for stance-taking. This spontaneous concept was particularly problematic given the context of mechanical engineering, where emotionally charged language (e.g. *huge, exciting, perfect*) that dramatically overstates or skews ideational accuracy regarding previous studies' empirical findings is discouraged, as evidenced in the instructor feedback collected during the needs analysis, if not entirely forbidden. Such a restricted conception of stance as primarily adjectival evaluation could lead students to incorrectly conclude that stance expressions are rare in their disciplinary writing, when in fact, stance is pervasively expressed through other

Table 8.1 Geyao's response to the definition activity before the tutoring

Name of the concept	Grammatical stance expression
Task prompt	In English Grammar, what is stance? What would you consider as stance expressions?
Before	In my opinion, the expression of stance usually includes the attitude and evaluation of the author toward the research/results. It can be conveyed to readers by some specific words.

Geyao's performance in sentence rewriting and corpus query activities.

linguistic means (authorial position and self-presence), which are central to a comprehensive understanding of academic stance. Additionally, Geyao lacked awareness of the distinction between propositional and metadiscoursal content, as well as discipline-specific guidelines for making appropriate claims in mechanical engineering research writing. The absence of concrete examples and specific usage rules further suggests that her understanding remained at a formal level, without the functional depth needed for effective implementation in academic writing.

Once participants completed their definition task prior to the instruction, they received a scientific presentation of the concept using the didactic models. Then, two materialization activities were in line to put them in a guided environment to apply the concept. As described in the preceding context chapter, the Sentence Rewriting activity gives them a number of complex sentences from the class corpus. Their task is to use the flowcharts as psychological tools for thinking to identify specific linguistic features based on learned concepts. In Grammatical Stance Expressions, this includes identifying and labeling stance expressions (see Figure 8.2) in a selected passage.

Different from definition data, the analysis here focuses on visual interactions with the materials during activity completion with supplementary reference to their written completion to check whether they approached the activity successfully or not. In completing this task, it was found in the screen recording that Geyao predominantly cohered with the instruction with high accuracy, although she primarily relied on the stance taxonomy handout and had little use of other materials, with only brief instances of referring to other resources. It shows a direct impact of instruction and quick uptake of the scientific conceptualization of stance expressions in the activity. It does not mean, however, that flowcharts were not made useful. In her post-intervention interview (Excerpt 8.1), she described how she used the flowchart of Intra-Sentence Discoursal Function to approach this activity:

Task 2: (1) Identify stance markers (including words, phrases and clauses) from the following paragraphs.
(2) Focus on stance complement clauses, identify position (neutral, hedging, boosting), evaluation (yes, no) and authorial presence (yes, no).
Note that this time they are all published writing samples.

1. To test, we developed a Monte Carlo simulation of a representative Army vehicle project. We first replicate prior studies without implementation delays, then incorporate delays for comparison. Once added, the value of flexibility degrades rapidly. The rate of degradation varies based on the flexibility strategy. Our results suggest a need to consider implementation uncertainty in evaluating flexible design options.

Figure 8.2 Geyao's task in sentence rewriting activity

Excerpt 8.1 Step by step through the flowchart

To find the clause, I followed the one we talked about before, um, look for that second verb other than the first one inside the main clause, and then right. I'm going to judge that type of its clause structure. [...] Start from the first step in the flowchart, and go down step by step, step by step). (Post-intervention interview)

In Grammatical Stance Expressions, the taxonomy handout could have provided a readily attuned reference for Geyao's developmental status and saved her from going through the multiple decision-making steps for reaching a conclusion, making it easier to navigate and apply efficiently to the Sentence Rewriting tasks. Nevertheless, her use of taxonomy handouts was mostly successful; she was able to reliably identify stance expressions in the chosen passage.

After this activity, Geyao engaged in the Corpus Query activity. This activity provided participants with step-by-step instructions to use AntConc for querying linguistic instances and answering related questions to match such instances with rhetorical functions in research writing. In Grammatical Stance Expressions, she was tasked with identifying top instances of stance complement clauses in the class corpus using AntConc (see Figure 8.3). The analysis focuses similarly on identifying areas of interesting dissonances, particularly instances of her labored query experience and off-task behavior, and exploring potential reasons supported by video analysis and post-intervention interview data.

As shown in her screen recording, she primarily engaged with the corpus tool AntConc, using it at various points to explore linguistic instances. In order to retrieve a stance complement clause from a corpus using AntConc, one has to harness the wildcard function (e.g. *, []) in AntConc and be aware that they have to capture the parts-of-speech forms of the controlling word. Some of these functionalities were introduced and practiced in early lessons, where she likened the corpus syntax search to literature search ('*In fact, this search, this square bracket and so on, are similar with the kind of literature searching in which to enter the key words*') and felt little trouble to learn because they are very similar to the more familiar advanced search of literature online.

Despite a largely coherent experience, right off the start of her query in AntConc, she had trouble interpreting the step-by-step instructions regarding the advanced search functionality. In Figure 8.4, she followed the steps to try and retrieve the noun-controlled *that*-clause. She stumbled at the advanced search where the list of context words should be input one by one instead of putting them in a string. This generated an error message in AntConc. She then took initiative to address this issue by herself by searching online what problem this refers to. Unfortunately, it did not return any positive results because AntConc debugging posts were not as popular as other software tools and the Google community

Task 3: Now try search stance complement clauses by yourself.
How do we find noun-, verb- and adjective-controlled complement clauses?
List top three verbs, nouns and adjectives controlling *that*-clause [(1)-(3)] and top three adjectives controlling (6).
(1) Noun-controlled *that*-clause
  1. Open ME_FULL_TAG.db file
  2. Check 'Adv Search'
  3. Check 'Context Search'
  4. Select Window Span from '0L' to '5R'
  5. Select 'Not in context'
  6. Add 'MD', 'VBD', 'VBP', 'VBZ', 'VBN'
  7. Click 'Apply'
  8. Adjust 'Sort 1' to 'C'
  9. Input '* NN* that' into the search box
  10. Run 'Start'
(2) Verb-controlled *that*-clause
  1. Open ME_FULL_TAG.db file
  2. Uncheck 'Adv Search'
  3. Choose 'C' from 'Sort 1'
  4. Input '* V* that' into the search box
  5. Run 'Start'
(3) Adjective-controlled *that*-clause
  1. Open ME_FULL_TAG.db file
  2. Adjust 'Sort 1' to 'C'
  3. Input '* JJ that' into the search box
  4. Run 'Start'

Figure 8.3 Geyao's task in corpus query activity

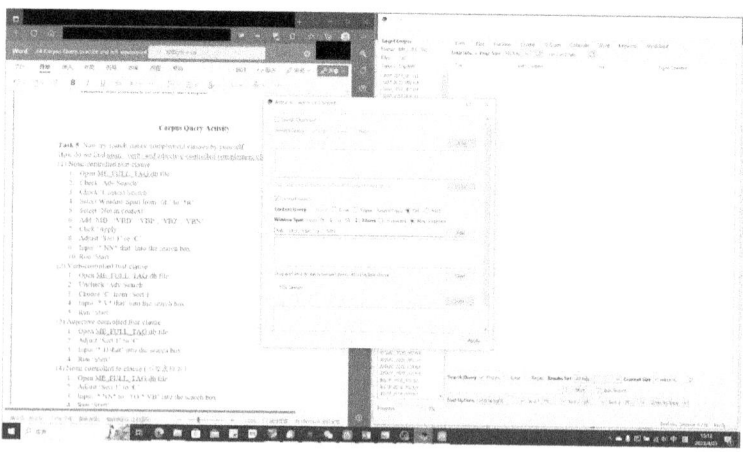

Figure 8.4 A screenshot of Geyao's advanced search using AntConc

that offered Q&A support for AntConc use (as maintained by the developer Dr Lawrence Anthony) was not accessible due to China's firewall policy. As the noun-controlled *that*-clause is the only linguistic category that involved advanced searches, Geyao was largely successful in obtaining the expected concordance lines by following the steps of other stance complement clauses. From the concordance lines, she sorted their frequency and reviewed the context of each instance to determine if it indeed functions as a stance expression.

Geyao's Verbalization in Self-Assessment Activities

After the materialization activities, Geyao engaged in a self-assessment activity which asked her to select two to three paragraphs from her first draft and informally identify and annotate the linguistic concept learned in class. In Grammatical Stance Expressions, Geyao needs to identify her stance use in various forms and verbalize their appropriateness based on the concept she learned and practiced in this instructional unit. At the post-intervention interview, Geyao appreciated the fact that this activity allowed for the use of her own writing as a site of linguistic inquiry through which she was able to verbalize her understanding of the learned concepts and reason its tool value to improving the quality of her manuscript (Excerpt 8.2). Expectedly, the kind of linguistic analysis involved in performing this activity drew broadly from trained skills – using flowcharts to map linguistic form to discoursal/rhetorical function and querying the pedagogic corpus to contextualize expressions against expert texts.

Excerpt 8.2 I paid more attention when it's my own writing

In the process of analysis, I found that there were a lot of problems. And then it's the revising that's just probably going to be a little bit more, just a little bit more laborious, I guess, and it's just that there's definitely a little bit more attention paid to this one compared to the other activities, because it's my own writing, after all. And then I thought about what methods I could use to improve it, and that might be a combination of the methods that I used to do tasks for other activities, so it just added up to a longer time. (Post-intervention interview)

In Grammatical Stance Expressions, Geyao independently identified instances of boosters, hedges, evaluatives, and self-mentions in her draft and then explained how some sentences can be improved. As shown in

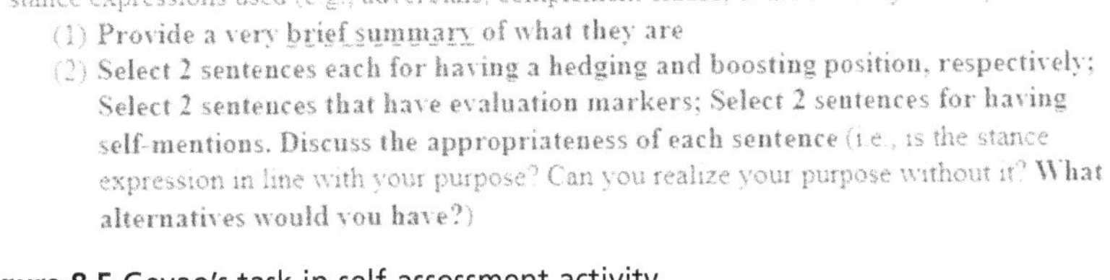

Self-assessment
Task 4. Select two paragraphs from your own writing and perform a manual analysis of the stance expressions used (e.g., adverbials, complement clause, evaluative adjectives). Please
(1) Provide a very brief summary of what they are
(2) Select 2 sentences each for having a hedging and boosting position, respectively; Select 2 sentences that have evaluation markers; Select 2 sentences for having self-mentions. Discuss the appropriateness of each sentence (i.e., is the stance expression in line with your purpose? Can you realize your purpose without it? What alternatives would you have?)

Figure 8.5 Geyao's task in self-assessment activity

Excerpt 8.3 from her handout, Geyao first provided example sentences from her first draft that contained stance expressions and then explained her choices in the identification. In the first part of her comment, Geyao quoted a sentence from her introduction where she employed a combination of hedging expressions and self-mentions to describe the limitations of current research and express her personal assessment of the situation. She further demonstrates this development when analyzing her use of boosters, observing how *'phrases such as is demand to and propose a novel strategy help position me stronger and more confidently.'* Her understanding extends to recognizing how stance markers work together, reflected in her insight that *'Without these stance expressions, it would be harder to show the need for research if it was just an objective description.'* Her ability to notice and analyze these features without explicit prompting indicates movement toward self-regulation in understanding stance. Her noticing that these linguistic choices are *'consistent with [her] purpose in terms of evaluation and position'* demonstrates that the concept of grammatical stance expressions was becoming a psychological tool for her writing development. Her emerging ability to connect these linguistic features to her goal of the paper within the disciplinary communication suggests development within her Zone of Proximal Development, moving from assisted to more autonomous control of these concepts.

Excerpt 8.3 Matching stance expressions with writing intentions

Boosters: For diatom biosilica-based NDDS, specific chemical modification **is demanded to** impart them with stimuli-responsive drug release capability within rhinitis-induced unique nasal environment (pH~5.0, 35 °C)[25].

Hedges: Typically, modification of diatom biosilica based on silane coupling agents and reactive linkers **tends to** have low synthesis and modification efficiency[26].

Self-mentions: In this study, **we proposed** a novel strategy of integrated modification on diatomite biosilica (DB) using polydopamine (PDA) and carboxymethyl chitosan (CMCS) to construct nasal drug vehicles for the first time.

Summary: The above examples are part of the introduction, which mainly describes the advantages of diatom as biotemplate material used in my research, as well as its current status and shortcomings in the application of carrier. In the introduction section, I intended to explain the purpose and significance of this study by stating that "Diatom biosilica is an excellent porous biotemplate material for the development of drug delivery systems, but the current research is limited to the oral form, and the synthesis efficiency of the relevant chemical modifications of diatoms is low". From the above analysis, I have the following discoveries when I was describing the personal position: (1) In the section on assessing the shortcomings of the current situation, the use of hedging expression and self-mention to describe the shortcomings and personal assessment of the current situation is consistent with my purpose in terms of perception and position. (2) In the section on proposing the significance and novelty of my research, expressions such as *is demand to*, *propose a novel strategy*, are used to present my position more confidently, which is in line with my writing intention. Without these stance expressions, it would be harder to show the need for research if it was just an objective description. (Grammatical Stance Expressions handout)

Geyao's definition at the end of the instruction

Immediately after the completion of the Self-Assessment activity, Geyao was asked again to define Grammatical Stance Expressions under the same task prompt. As shown in Table 8.2, she demonstrated noticeable progress in her grasp of the concept. The definition integrated considerations like hedging, boosting, employing active/passive voice judiciously – principles aligned with the scientific presentation. This suggested an emerging recognition of key disciplinary tenets related to stance and making scientifically rigorous claims. While her linguistic choices continued to reflect a detached stance similar to her previous definition, these choices represented conscious decisions about her positioning in academic discourse. Her stance from '*In my opinion*' to '*I personally believe*' maintained a tentative positioning, and her use of phrases such as '*the author should use*' suggested she was agentively choosing to discuss stance from an observer's perspective. This positioning (conscious or otherwise), though not aligned with target disciplinary conventions, demonstrates her exercise of agency in making discourse choices, even as she worked to internalize new concepts about academic stance-taking. While Geyao performed competently in materialization activities with minimal didactic support, suggesting she could operate the concepts independently, her persistent

Table 8.2 Geyao's response to the definition activity immediately after the tutoring

Name of the concept	Grammatical stance expression
Task prompt	In English Grammar, what is stance? What would you consider as stance expressions?
After	I personally believe that in ME writing, personal stance represents the author's attitude and judgment (confidence) about the research results/status quo, and an author should use hedging or boosting expression appropriately to accurately convey the research results/status quo. At the same time, the use of active/passive sentences should also pay attention to its scientific nature.

observer stance raises questions about genuine internalization. Rather than indicating autonomy, her reduced need for psychological tools to mediate materialized actions might reflect a more superficial understanding – one that allows task completion without true conceptual appropriation.

The possibility that Geyao simply reproduced course content to create a scientifically acceptable definition becomes more plausible when considering the sequence of the learning activities. Both the Sentence Rewriting and Self-Assessment tasks required identification of specific stance elements (position, evaluation, and self-mention), which appeared nearly verbatim in her definition. Given these observations, claims about her development following the intended trajectory remain inconclusive. Further insight into this question emerges in the analysis of her post-intervention revision process and recalls, as is discussed below.

Geyao's Verbalization in Stimulated Recalls for Post-Intervention Revisions

After completing the tutoring sessions, participants were given two weeks to revise their original drafts and record their revision process using screen capture software. The goal of this revision was to improve their manuscripts to a publication-ready state that their advisors would approve for journal submission. These screen recordings later served as stimuli for recall sessions conducted within a week of submission. Using these recordings, Qiu developed a heuristic to analyze revision behaviors at both linguistic levels (such as word additions and deletions) and discourse levels (such as finding language equivalents or searching for alternatives). For one participant, Geyao, her engagement with various resources provided insight into her evolving understanding and articulation of linguistic concepts during writing. These resources ranged from her existing knowledge (cognitive resources) to linguistic materials (handouts and flowcharts), model papers, online translation tools, and corpus analysis software (AntConc). While all participants primarily relied on their cognitive resources to address identified issues during revision, Geyao stood out in her more frequent use of AntConc. She demonstrated confidence in applying her conceptual understanding of sentence-level linguistics before seeking external help and showed willingness to experiment with new digital tools to verify her choices. Her typical revision process followed these steps: identifying problems, formulating solutions while consulting various materials (as illustrated in Figure 8.6), evaluating the results from these materials, and finally enacting the revisions.

A noticeable learning outcome was her newly developed revision pattern of cross-validation. This was particularly evident when she encountered uncertainty or dissatisfaction with outcomes from other resources. As shown in Table 8.3, during the drafting phase, Geyao frequently used the verb '*verify*' to describe her experimental procedures, adopting this usage from a model paper published by a colleague in her research group.

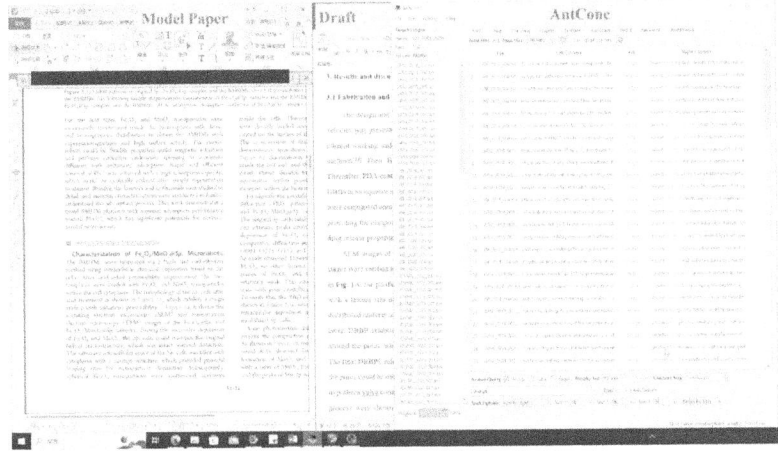

Figure 8.6 A screenshot of Geyao's real-time materialized action during the post-Intervention revision activity

Table 8.3 Can SEM be verified?: An example of Geyao's problem-solving strategy

Strategy	Description	Verbalization
Detect a problem	'SEM images … were **verified** to characterize the morphology and structure.' (First Draft)	I picked up the use of 'verify' in one model paper during drafting. Now I look at it, I don't think SEM images were 'verified' to do this. It's not what I meant, but I don't have alternatives in my mind.
Formulate a solution	Consult external resources	
Choose a tool	AntConc	I wanted to know what experts describe about SEM images and see what verbs they choose.
Perform a search	'images' (AntConc)	
Evaluate a query		There are more than 200 hits. I can't find one relevant to SEM.
Perform a search	'SEM' (AntConc)	
Evaluate a query	'…, the detailed surface morphology of the as-built part was also observed using an SEM.' (AntConc)	There are 28 hits. And I spotted one with the verb I was looking for. Its context of use is very similar to mine.
Perform a search	'observe|observed' (AntConc)	I wanted to also make sure the tense of this verb is also appropriate
Evaluate a query		The passive form is way more often than the active form, so I figured that a passive construction is preferred in my discipline.
Revise	[Replace] 'SEM images … were **observed** to characterize the morphology and structure.' (Final Draft)	
Evaluate the revision		I think I've made the right choice.

Note. '()' indicates the source of the quoted text. '[]' indicates revision type.

She initially saw no issue with this choice, given its presence in the published work. However, after the intervention, which emphasized identifying clause types through verb recognition, she became more attentive to her verb usage. As she noted in her post-intervention interview, '*I remembered your introduction of English clause that when you see a verb, you also see a clause.*' This heightened awareness led her to examine her word choices more carefully, applying her new understanding of linguistic concepts and consulting the class corpus to find discipline-appropriate alternatives when needed. In analyzing '*verify,*' she recognized during her recall session that this verb typically requires a hypothesis and carries a definitive stance that she felt was unsuitable for her context.

Importantly, Geyao's goal extended beyond finding a simple synonym – she specifically sought a verb that would appropriately describe SEM (Scanning Electron Microscope) images within their syntactic context. While this might appear to be a minor word-level revision, her ability to explicitly identify and articulate this linguistic issue demonstrates a functional grasp of the four linguistic concepts introduced during tutoring, particularly Grammatical Stance Expressions, and her capacity to apply this knowledge in new, goal-oriented contexts. As Lantolf (2011a) and Lantolf and Poehner (2014) emphasize, this development indicates both the formation of a psychological tool for navigating genre practices and the potential for continued growth. Using her newly acquired tools, Geyao accessed discipline-specific usage patterns by examining how domain experts employed SEM-related terminology in the class corpus. As shown in Figure 8.7, her AntConc query for '*SEM*' yielded a number of concordance hits, allowing her to analyze the co-occurring verbs and their syntactic environments. This systematic approach to phrase hunting proved more effective and reliable than depending on a single model paper, which returned a satisfactory outcome.

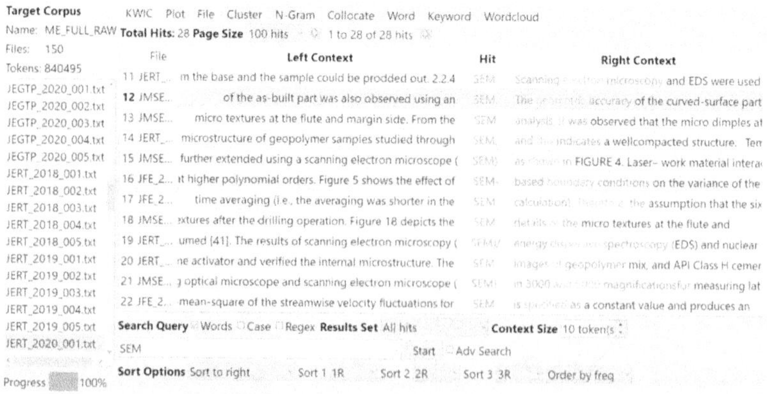

Figure 8.7 A screenshot of concordance hits of 'SEM' in Geyao's revision process

As also evidenced in most of Geyao's AntConc search patterns during revision, her consultation to the class corpus included attempts with verbs such as *'endow,' 'provide,' 'impart,' 'confer,'* and *'give,'* drawn from her academic reading experiences as potential alternatives for communicating the rhetorical purpose of describing her research findings. When participants closely emulate the structure, language, and rhetorical patterns found in model papers, especially those from within their own labs or from senior colleagues, there is a risk that their work may not sufficiently diverge or innovate beyond these examples. In other words, they would submit to mechanical mimicking instead of intelligent imitation (Negueruela, 2003). Imitation in the Vygotskian sense, 'exhibits a recombinatory aspect that may include imitating words or even morphemes, but juxtaposing them in ways that are novel, experimental, purposeful, and unique' (Lantolf & Yáñez, 2003: 100).

During the composition of her first draft before the tutoring, Geyao had committed to mimicking a list of publishable research-related verbs for ready use, not fully appreciating the rhetorical environments that frame the appropriate use of each verb in her specific discipline. Comparing her initial draft's verbs to those in a model paper she consulted during revision revealed at least 10 shared verb types, including *'exhibit'* (16 times), *'observe'* (13 times), *'conduct'* (7 times), *'verify'* (5 times), *'analyze'* (5 times), and *'investigate'* (5 times). Recognizing the importance of adhering to discipline-specific norms, she voiced concerns about her repetitive verb choices and needed a way to cross-validate the appropriateness of alternatives in ME research article writing, a task that only this tutoring seemed to effectively tackle. Moreover, the precise context in which these verbs are appropriately used in ME writing remained partial to her until she was introduced to the linguistic concepts and the corpus analysis.

Her post-intervention interview response (Excerpt 8.4) further validates this development. Particularly notable was her evolution from surface-level emulation to deeper rhetorical awareness: *'Before the tutoring, I simply emulated its content . . . but I did not follow its line of logic flow, especially the sentence emphasis.'* Her description of moving from *'simply put[ting] all the information I wanted to put in there, without a good logic'* to consciously analyzing how model texts use *'sentence form to bring out the point it emphasizes'* demonstrates a qualitative transformation in her approach. She now recognizes the rhetorical function of specific linguistic features, noting how elements such as *'however'* can 'highlight what limitations the current research has' and strategically lead into her own research. This evolution from mechanical information presentation to strategic engagement with rhetorical structures exemplifies Vygotsky's notion of higher mental functioning, where learned concepts become tools for conscious control over cognitive activity.

Excerpt 8.4 From simply emulating content to conscious logic flow

Before the tutoring, I simply emulated its (the model paper) content, that is, for example, its first paragraph with a few sentences, but I did not follow its line of logic flow, especially the sentence emphasis. Now I consciously pay attention to how it is through the sentence form to bring out the point it emphasizes. Before tutoring, I simply put all the information I wanted to put in there, without a good logic. For example, at the beginning of writing the Introduction, I just divided what I thought into a few paragraphs and wrote it up, but later on when I was revising, I would find that it is after saying that literature overview first, you have to highlight one of your novelties at the end, such as having a 'however', or through a kind of an emphasis to highlight what limitations the current research has at the moment, and then lead appropriately into your research. That is, there will be an improvement on my logic. Before tutoring it might just mean laying out all the information. (Post-

Geyao's Definition at the Delayed Interview

Two months after the stimulated recall sessions, participants completed a follow-up interview with Qiu to assess their sustained conceptual development. This interview included a definition task, a corpus query activity, and a semi-structured interview. Geyao's response to the definition task of Grammatical Stance Expressions, shown in Table 8.4, reveals significant development in her understanding and personalization of the Grammatical Stance Expression concept. Most striking in Geyao's delayed response is her shift toward more agentive language, indicating deeper internalization of the concept. Rather than providing a detached, textbook-style definition that she did immediately after the tutoring, she

Table 8.4 Geyao's response to the definition activity two months after the tutoring

Name of the concept	Grammatical stance expression
Task prompt	In English Grammar, what is stance? What would you consider as stance expressions?
Delayed	Stance is a concept that I use less often, but I have found that it is mainly reflected in four aspects: the first one is whether my draft is in active or passive voice, whether the use of modal verbs is appropriate, and whether my personal opinion is appropriate in the evaluation and in the description of other people's work, and then whether my sentence structure conveys my personal attitude or my accurate judgment on the results. I think it's more important in these areas, first of all, the appropriateness of your vocabulary choices of boosting, neutral or hedging and the way in which you express your personal opinion, and then presenting the work you personally do, and whether you are using the self-mention or the more objective passive voice. Studying this concept will better help me to restructure my essay and evaluate my position in terms of the soundness and logic of my research.

articulated the concept through the lens of her own writing practice. This is evident in phrases such as '*my draft,*' '*whether my sentence structure conveys my personal attitude,*' and how '*studying this concept will better help me to restructure my essay.*' Such personal framing suggests she has moved beyond merely understanding the rules to actively engaging with the concept as a tool for making rhetorical choices in her writing. Her response demonstrated a comprehensive understanding of the concept's core elements, including modal verbs, voice selection, and the appropriate evaluation of others' work. She also emphasized the strategic use of boosting and hedging devices, and the intentional choice between self-mention and passive voice constructions. The evolution in Geyao's conceptual understanding is particularly evident in how she frames stance as a decision-making tool. Her response suggests that the concept has become a flexible psychological tool through which to evaluate and calibrate her claims. This development aligns with Concept-Based Genre Writing pedagogy's emphasis on empowering learners to make discourse-appropriate choices independently. Her ability to not only retain but expand upon her initial understanding demonstrates how the concept has become integrated into her writing practice as a dynamic tool rather than remaining a static set of rules.

Conclusion

Geyao's journey from initial formal awareness to eventual internalization demonstrates how conceptual development can empower learners for agentive participation in disciplinary writing practices. At the outset, Geyao's everyday understanding was limited to basic recognition of attitudinal expressions, primarily focused on evaluative adjectives. Through the concept presentation and materialization phases, she demonstrated quick uptake of the scientific conceptualization, successfully identifying stance expressions in model texts and corpus data. Her engagement with Self-Assessment Activities marked an important transition, as she began applying these concepts to analyze her own writing, showing emerging ability to connect linguistic features to rhetorical goals within her discipline's genre practices. The post-intervention revision process further revealed perhaps the most compelling evidence of development toward the Concept-Based Genre Writing pedagogy goal of empowering learners for locally responsive decision-making. Geyao evolved from mechanical mimicking of model papers to implementing a thoughtful cross-validation strategy, using linguistic concepts to detect a problem in her writing and using corpus analysis to verify appropriate verb choices. Her approach to revision demonstrated growing metalinguistic awareness and strategic use of resources. While her immediate post-instruction definition showed comprehensive knowledge but remained somewhat detached, her delayed definition two months later revealed deeper internalization through more agentive language. She moved from describing stance as an abstract concept to articulating it as a practical tool for making rhetorical choices in her own writing. Critically, Geyao's development manifested the Concept-Based Genre Writing pedagogy core principle that learner agency is both the goal of and evidence of development. Her growing ability to make intentional, principled choices about stance expressions – whether adhering to or thoughtfully departing from disciplinary conventions – demonstrated that when properly mediated through carefully designed pedagogical tools and responsive instruction, complex linguistic concepts can become internalized resources for autonomous, discourse-appropriate decision-making in disciplinary writing.

9 Implications and Considerations for Other Contexts

The preceding chapters have motivated and exemplified a Concept-Based Genre Writing pedagogy. Our aim in bringing these projects together was to showcase the applicability of the framework and its profound potential to empower and equip learners for future writing. These studies targeted diverse focal concepts to transform learner understanding of and participation in distinct genre practices, and they were implemented in distinct contexts with diverse multilingual student populations. The interventions also showcase a range of approaches to presenting and materializing concepts, shaping educational activity around verbalization and performance, implementing unique didactic models, and providing arenas for social mediation. These studies also collected data to analyze learner development through a variety of means. Yet, in the development and implementation of the studies reside profound commonalities, not least of which is our shared commitment to be responsible educators. Through the lenses of the three premises around which we motivate our Concept-Based Genre Writing pedagogy in Chapter 2, these projects were *transformationally projected toward the future,* placed *learner agency as the goal of development and evidence of development,* and *targeted locally responsive decision-making.* That is, each study focused on learners' agentive decisions in literacy activity and viewed articulable reasons for writerly decisions as both the end goal of the instruction and evidence of development towards that goal. Each study valued student awareness of how competing demands in context affected student decision-making in their writing – in contextualized, situated thinking, rather than as rules of thumb and formulas.

In Chapters 3 and 4, Kurtz's intervention aimed to develop core disciplinary reasoning skills with immediate local importance for navigating legal education and high-stakes written genre practices. The concept, legal analogical reasoning, affords students longer-term access to legal reasoning and access to analytical frames described by disciplinary experts as thinking like a lawyer. In this regard, the course does not focus on classroom-bound skills or formulas for solving cases. Rather, it aims to equip learners with psychological tools that grant greater access to legal pedagogy, enable meaningful engagement with legal problems, and project towards participation in cognitive and discursive forms of legal reasoning and activity. By the end of the study, students demonstrated greater ability to identify how analogical reasoning as a way of disciplinary thinking shaped the genres they both read and wrote and greater control over appropriating that disciplinary thinking into their own participation in written legal discourse.

In Chapters 5 and 6, Casal showcased how multilingual graduate student writers' internalization of two concepts (a subset of those in the pedagogy) transformed the way that these students thought about, conceptualized, and engaged in academic writing practices. The pedagogy aimed to support graduate student writers from across disciplines in physical science, social science, and humanities, with an emphasis both on their current academic projects as a site for meaningful application of evolving understandings and projection toward the future and developing academic identities. Through a focus on the genre-specific functional affordances and meaning-potentials of linguistic features, as well as genre-specific rhetorical actions, the pedagogy led to the transformative emergence of nascent and developing agentive, socially conscious, and rhetorically intentional authorial identity. Graduate student writers demonstrated marked re-orientation to academic research writing from initial conceptualizations based on grammaticality and subject matter towards a more complex view of genre practices as strategic, rhetorical, and dialogically social.

In Chapters 7 and 8, Qiu demonstrated how L1 Chinese graduate students developed their English research writing skills in Mechanical Engineering during a remote writing tutoring. Drawing on a needs analysis from engineering writing textbooks, instructor feedback, and corpus-based comparison between expert and student writing, the pedagogy identified four critical sentence-level linguistic concepts as the instructional focus. Through flowchart-based didactic models to visualize these concepts, along with a systematic sequence of materialization activities including sentence rewriting, corpus query, and self-assessment tasks, the pedagogy captured both the participants' immediate interaction with pedagogical materials and broader developmental trajectories. Participants were no longer merely following the rules taught in prior English education. Instead, they have been equipped with the conceptual resources for diagnosing their writing and developed a keener sense of what to look for, such as the appropriateness of flow, emphasis, and stance.

Emerging Points of Intersection

We find more local commonalities and intersecting themes across both the learners' developmental journeys and our own growth in coming to work with learners within a Concept-Based Genre Writing pedagogy framework. Not least among these was the considerable effort involved in the pedagogies and the tremendous growth we experienced through them. In this section, we discuss points of intersection across the interventions discussed in this volume.

Concept-Based Genre Writing pedagogy as a continuum

It is important for us to reflect on the scalability, feasibility, and openness of a Concept-Based Genre Writing pedagogy, and we do so through a discussion of the variability the pedagogy affords in practice. As a starting point, we acknowledge that there is considerable variation in the amount of control that writing instructors have over what genres and concepts make it into a syllabus, how class time is structured, and how development is assessed formally. To this end, we note that we all enjoyed tremendous freedom to shape educational activity in our contexts, even as our constraints were variable. While Casal had (nearly) complete freedom in developing a writing course and curriculum around academic research writing genres and linguistic/rhetorical concepts, Kurtz developed an intervention for analogical reasoning to fit within a broader legal curriculum, and Qiu developed an extracurricular language module for engineering research writing. In all cases, their interventions were innovatively developed around the constraints and affordances of their educational situations and learners within their contexts. Likewise, and in part in response to characteristics of context, Kurtz's intervention was framed most directly through C-BLI, Casal's intervention foregrounded genre, and Qiu's intervention is the most balanced integration.

Mediating the mediation

An important consideration in thinking about the scalability of Concept-Based Genre Writing pedagogy is the extent to which different forms of mediation interact with each other. In each project in this volume, we observe occasions of one form of mediation being mediated by another. That is, each of us developed conceptual mediation for our studies, and provided social mediation to students. We additionally acknowledge the prior and outside mediational forces acting on student thinking. The interaction of these mediational forces often required further mediation. These interactions include contact between conceptual mediation and conceptual mediation, concepts and other concepts, conceptual mediation and social mediation, and social mediation and social mediation.

Students working with multiple forms of conceptual mediation when engaged in practical, goal-oriented activity must make decisions about which conceptual mediation suits their in-the-moment needs. We see this vividly in Qiu's data where Geyao primarily oriented to one form of conceptual mediation, the taxonomy handout for stance expressions, over other forms, where Qiu points out that her typically preferred conceptual mediation would have more efficiently helped her decision-making process than plodding her way through the flowchart. Whereas, she found the flowchart more useful for the intra-sentence discoursal functions in rewriting activity because of its visual representation of hierarchical relationships between clauses. When students are provided multiple forms of rich conceptual mediation, part of the developmental journey will be learning how to use the conceptual mediation in goal-oriented activity. That is, evidence of development in a phase where students still rely on conceptual mediation may very well be their ability to choose which tool solves which problem for them.

In studies where more than one concept is taught, as in Casal's course, considering how concepts interact with each other will be important for scalability of the framework. For example, one of Casal's focal students, Mona, does not immediately orient to how a conceptual understanding of rhetorical moves could transform her relationship to academic writing. As the course progressed and further concepts were introduced, suddenly, as if a critical mass threshold had been reached, Mona sees rhetorical moves everywhere and as transformative. Here, the concepts built the social dimensions of writing (e.g. stance and rhetoric) on each other until, through the morass of stars, Mona metaphorically saw the constellation. We consider scalability not merely important for thinking about concept sequencing, but also the point at which quantitative accumulation of ideas turns into qualitative change in learners as concepts build on each other. The V-SCT grounding of our framework suggests that this change is likely to come in fits and starts, through moments of upheaval.

Naturally, in the course of teaching, conceptual mediation and social mediation interact, and the strength of one is the weakness of the other. Working with SCOBAs (conceptual mediation) requires sustained, although always dynamic, mediation as students develop familiarity with using them meaningfully as a tool. Other times, when conceptual mediation diverges sharply from students' prior educational histories, social mediation usefully guides students as they use conceptual mediation. For example, in Kurtz's study, students occasionally oriented to legal cases through their prior legal training to the extent that the pedagogical goals of US legal education became obscured. In such cases, re-orienting to what the pedagogical purpose of the conceptual mediation (e.g. *what are these cases put into these books to teach us?*) focused the instructional conversation in a way that allowed the student to use the conceptual mediation more effectively. That is, through social mediation, the conceptual mediation became a more effective tool for the student.

Finally, in the fluid, messy, dynamic environment of many writing classrooms, social mediation will interact with social mediation. Casal's focal student Lucía represents a powerful example of this. Her play with the metalanguage (e.g. through her *freeze it and front it* tagline) and concepts taught in the class mediated not only her own thoughts, but also positively affected the classroom dynamic, with her taglines ultimately serving as another form of mediation for fellow classmates. This is to say that student reactions to the social mediation offered by teachers can provide additional, also powerful social mediation for both themselves and their peers.

Presence of all phases in nearly all activity

The chapters provide strong evidence that the six phases of C-BLI were interwoven throughout various activities rather than occurring in a strict stage-by-stage sequence. In Kurtz's legal writing study, participants' pre-understanding, as first elicited through analysis of their home legal systems, permeated through the entire Reading Role cycle. Moreover, they had continual access to the materializations, each received physical copies of the SCOBAs to use as they analyzed legal problems. The mediation sessions further illustrated this phase integration when Jun struggled with case-concept connections in the second IRAC essay, combining the dissonance between his pre-understanding and initial concept presentation, materialization through the SCOBAs, languaging through discussion with the instructor, and performance through legal analysis. In Casal's graduate writing study, Mona's case particularly illustrates how pre-understanding can persistently interact with other phases. She entered the course with a deeply held view of writing as primarily about '*grammar*' and '*clarity*.' This pre-understanding was so entrenched that it initially led to resistance during concept presentations. A turning point came in Week 6 when she suddenly recognized that '*everything is a move*' and that 'there are all these things that the writer is trying to do.' She was verbalizing her understanding through discussion with her partner, performing concept analysis by identifying moves in text, actively challenging her previous conception, and using the materialized moves framework to make sense of the texts before her. Importantly, her pre-understanding remained actively engaged in this process but was now being reconstructed through her new rhetorical awareness. In Qiu's engineering writing context, this integration was evident particularly in self-assessment activities, as students drew on their pre-understanding through their own drafts, performed concept identification, verbalized their analysis process, and demonstrated internalization by applying concepts to their writing. In Geyao's analysis of stance expressions in her introduction, she worked to reconcile her growing conceptual understanding with her actual writing practices by performing multiple concept-related tasks simultaneously while verbalizing the rationale behind these choices. Across these contexts, we believe that an effective Concept-Based Genre Writing pedagogy should focus not on shepherding learners through sequential phases but on creating rich opportunities for learners to productively wrestle with concepts through various modes of engagement simultaneously.

Learner perceptions of growth

Development is central to all work in a Vygotskian tradition and is foregrounded in the various approaches to genre-based writing pedagogies, but our interventions highlight a particular theme in considerations of learner development: learner perceptions of growth. In this regard, we note two important points. First, within both studies targeting academic research writing, student self-perceptions of development are mediated by the evaluations of doctoral dissertation advisors in powerful ways. In both studies, we did not ask students to share or reflect on experiences with their doctoral advisors, and yet prior and ongoing mentoring experiences were referenced as touchstones of development, such that the significance of advisor–advisee relationships in framing orientation to academic research writing and notions of self-efficacy were profound. Casal found that students were often quick to report feeling more confident in discussing or identifying target concepts, and they over time reported more intentionality in their decision-making as writers, but they were unsure of their own improvement *as writers* until their doctoral advisors commented as such. Both case study participants discussed in Chapter 6 make direct reference to their advisors' perceptions at the beginning and end of the term without being prompted. Importantly, these two students frame strongly supportive and positive relationships with their advisors. Qiu found one of his participants' orientation to writing to be so profoundly shaped by negative experiences with their advisor's evaluative judgments that it sharply limited their perceptions of agency as a writer.

Moving to the second point, the pedagogy led to observable development from a research perspective, but this development was also tangible and transformational in the learners' own self-perceptions. Returning to Qiu's context, the pedagogy allowed for this and other students to reclaim agency in decision-making, and in Casal's context, Lucía used both rhetorical moves and shell noun concepts to structure and organize discussions of writing *with* her advisor. Kurtz's students not only demonstrated their internalization of analogical reasoning, but they also reported feeling more capable of and prepared to participate in law classes beyond the intervention through the new psychological tools they had acquired. That is, they were aware of and felt transformationally empowered by developing capacities to engage in disciplinary thinking in ways that shaped evolving professional identities.

Learning is revolutionary

The learners' developmental trajectories reported in our studies fundamentally challenge notions of smooth, linear progression in learning. This supports a diverse array of theoretical approaches to second language learning development that predict non-linear development. In analyzing development as 'upheavals,' we specifically looked for moments when students' conceptual understanding appeared to shift dramatically or seemingly regress as potential indicators of genuine development. Jun in Kurtz's legal writing case study attempted analogical reasoning early in the semester but did so superficially, writing separate paragraphs for precedent and current cases without an analogical connection. By mid-semester, he appeared to regress, abandoning analogical reasoning entirely in his second IRAC essay. This regression actually indicated a productive disruption in his understanding as he was grappling with how to connect cases to concepts meaningfully, rather than simply reproducing the form of analogical reasoning (e.g. signal language) without conceptual understanding. Therefore, it marked a crucial destabilization period where, significantly, he could complete legal analogical reasoning when socially mediated by Kurtz in his third IRAC. By his final IRAC, he developed further by producing legal analogical reasoning in independent written performance for the first time and demonstrating the ability to see both sides of legal arguments orally.

Mona in Casal's graduate writing class first demonstrated an understanding of shell nouns (correctly identifying their cohesive function) but then retreated to jokes about not being able to use them herself. A major upheaval occurred in Week 6 with her 'everything is a move' revelation, yet there was not a steady rise thereafter. She initially responded by mechanically applying the rhetorical move framework to her conference abstract, which seemed to regress to a formula-based understanding. Yet, she began seeing moves as tools for reader awareness through her peer interaction and instructor-mediated discussion, leading to her innovative use of poem verses in her final paper specifically to make her work more rhetorically accessible to non-academic readers she hoped to reach. In Qiu's engineering writing, Geyao, in two in-class performance activities, demonstrated high accuracy in identifying stance expressions, and successfully retrieved stance complement clauses from the class corpus. In the self-assessment activity that followed, she demonstrated high-quality rhetorical analysis of stance in her writing, identifying and explaining how boosters, hedges, and self-mentions served specific research needs beyond objective description. However, when asked to define the concept again, she maintained a more detached position through observer-stance language that appeared to regress from a more agentive standpoint. This apparent regression was temporary, as her subsequent revision process revealed increasingly deliberate stance analysis. She articulated clear rationales for her revisions based not just on form, but on conscious consideration of author positioning and disciplinary expectations. By her delayed interview, Geyao had transformed her understanding, framing the concept through agentive language focused on her own writing.

Practical Questions for Practice

In what follows, we share suggestions for developing Concept-Based Genre Writing pedagogy in other contexts. We start with identifying what to teach, then discuss putting Concept-Based Genre Writing pedagogy into practice in the classroom and conclude with thoughts on reflection and refinement of an intervention for use with subsequent groups of students. We frame these discussions around the important consideration that everything is localized. The concepts and genres are closely intertwined, the pedagogy is framed around and responsive to learners' prior knowledge and current abilities, and the aim is agency in weighing local factors in making situated communicative decisions in target genre practices. We organize this section around questions educators may ask themselves and respond with practical answers.

How do I select the genre(s) to teach?

Identifying meaningful genres for a writing course is a major consideration, especially when teaching in disciplinary contexts or dealing with increasingly networked and multimodal genres. When students seek writing advice for their 'essays' or 'reports', these broad terms often mask distinctly different genres that serve various purposes across disciplines (Nesi & Gardner, 2012). Instead, our Concept-Based Genre Writing pedagogy emphasizes a needs-oriented approach that focuses on identifying and incorporating the specific types of writing that learners will encounter in their target situations. For instance, a legal writing course might address the range of oral and written genres used in law firms, while a writing course for graduate students in mechanical engineering might cover technical genres such as material inventories, technical reports, experimental notes, progress reports, and project proposals.

While a comprehensive needs analysis – involving student and instructor interviews, document collection, and classroom observations (e.g. Molle & Prior, 2008) – is ideal, we recognize that such extensive ethnographic research is not always feasible nor necessary for practical purposes. However, even small steps toward understanding student needs can be valuable. A good starting point could be as simple as a coffee or tea chat with someone who has either taught similar audiences or worked in the target context, including alumni. These conversations can not only illuminate relevant genres but also point towards valuable resources like conferences, book series, and pedagogical materials. For example, Qiu's consultation with an engineering education researcher affiliated with the

Department of Mechanical Engineering not only provided insights into relevant genres but also facilitated access to pedagogical opportunities for future interventions. Alternatively, if direct contacts are unavailable or unresponsive, you can implement a diagnostic survey that probes students' writing experiences and linguistic backgrounds before the beginning of a class. Online resources or organizations are also useful. They offer platforms where you can access course materials that were uploaded by other instructors and join reading groups or special interest groups to share needs and gather insights. Importantly, needs analysis is not a one-time task but an ongoing process. As Belcher (2006: 135) emphasizes, 'needs assessment itself [is] in need of continual reassessment'. Your understanding of appropriate genres should evolve as you become more familiar with your student population and their writing contexts.

How do I identify a concept for C-BLI?

Concept selection is an important, if daunting, step in C-BLI. Candidates for target concepts can primarily be identified in two places – a teacher's experience and the scholarly literature. Teachers know the curriculum they teach and are well-positioned to identify core concepts students need to master in their contexts, as well as areas of the curriculum that are notoriously 'sticky' for students. Core concepts should orient students to knowledge that will project them toward futures where they agentively make decisions about meaning-making in familiar and novel contexts. In the context of teacher education, Esteve *et al.* (2021) define core concepts in that domain as 'scientific concepts that are essential ... to gain a deep understanding of [domain-specific knowledge] and to act informedly from a sociocultural perspective' (2021: 28). Notoriously difficult (or *sticky spots*) in the curriculum are also ripe for identifying concepts for C-BLI. These sticky spots are a good place to start because the struggle can indicate that perhaps the curriculum is not presenting a core idea holistically or conceptually. Core concepts and concepts students struggle to master are excellent places to start when identifying focal concept candidates for C-BLI.

Another source for identifying concepts is the scientific literature. Research can provide not only the definitions for concepts, but sometimes the concepts themselves. For example, many writing courses teach citation, often as a set of formal rules, perhaps with an accompanying explanation of *why we cite*. These explanations can cause students to believe that citation is arbitrary or undertaken only to avoid accusations of plagiarism. Citation in and of itself is not a scientific concept, but the research on intertextuality is. A unit introducing citation through the concept of intertextuality can help students make agentive decisions not only about how and where to cite, but provide them with deep knowledge as to how citation builds intertextual links. Within genre analysis, considerable research also directly identifies linguistic features that play prominent roles in genre practices and disciplinary activity.

How do I develop a holistic and complete definition of a concept?

In C-BLI, it is often said that scientific concepts are abstract, systematic, and generalizable; they are found in scientific literature, broadly defined. We recognize, however, that there are pragmatic limitations on resources like time, energy, and financial or material resources. In many contemporary C-BLI studies, teacher-researchers pair the pedagogical insights from C-BLI with meaning-based theories of language, such as cognitive linguistics or usage-based linguistics. In fact, the focus on meaning-making and agentive social action is why each of us finds genre-based pedagogy to be such a powerful partner for C-BLI. Guided by questions about how meaning is made with a scientific concept or sticky spot in the curriculum, we encourage teachers to seek out the best information available to them at the time to define the concept. C-BLI orients us to scientific literature, broadly understood, for these definitions, but it does not require that each and every implementation be perfect. We find the best, meaning-making-based definitions our time and resources allow us access to, and we develop conceptual materials around that definition, with the understanding that our own understandings of the concepts and their real-world application will develop over time. In a sense, this approach trusts teachers to enact the scientific method in their classrooms.

How related are the concepts to the genres in pedagogy?

The concepts should not merely be interesting ways for thinking about or orienting to a genre practice, they should be central components of effective participation in the target practice, or otherwise highly useful for such participation. By way of example, in Kurtz's pedagogical intervention, analogical reasoning is not an optional component of legal reasoning for successful participation in written US legal analysis. Rather, it is a psychological tool which frames the fundamental cognitive activity. In this sense, the concept is difficult, if impossible to divorce from the target genre activity, or a community-based family of legal genre activities. In many other cases, concepts may be essential for a given genre practice, but not necessarily uniquely associated with the practice. For example, in Qiu's pedagogical intervention, clausal subordination was the target concept for Mechanical Engineering research article writing. Clearly, clausal subordination is not unique to this genre practice. As can be seen from the pedagogy, explicit schematic information regarding clausal subordination is presented to learners from a structural linguistic perspective, but it is quickly localized to the functional affordances and meaning-making potentials within research writing context.

How do I develop a SCOBA?

As a starting point, it should be acknowledged that developing SCOBAs is neither easy nor formulaic. Two instructors teaching analogical reasoning could create SCOBAs very different in their appearance for their students that work perfectly well in their context. What is important in developing SCOBAs is that they coherently demonstrate the concept visually because they provide conceptual mediation that pairs with the verbal definition for use in actual activity. Since SCOBAs are intended to be used by students, so long as they need the mediation, in goal-based activity, SCOBAs must be actually usable by students. For example, Qiu's students found his SCOBAs intuitively usable because as engineers, they oriented to using flowcharts in their learning activity. Thus, the demands of the particular concept(s) under study, holistic representation of the concept, teacher orientation to the material, and student use of the mediation must all be balanced in the development of SCOBAs. This is to say, SCOBAs should represent visually the concept, but their form and their use can be different depending on the teaching-learning context.

In past C-BLI, SCOBAs have taken diverse forms, including those which could be described as mind maps, flowcharts, and pictures, as well as physical objects such as Cuissenaire rods or student manipulation of clay. SCOBAs can even be used in different phases of Concept-Based Genre Writing pedagogy. Teachers prepare SCOBAs for students to work with in practical, goal-based activity, but students may also be asked to create their own SCOBAs in a languaging or performance phase so that teachers can gain access to students' understanding of the concept(s) under study. Additionally, SCOBAs are an excellent place to seek input from colleagues and students. After developing a SCOBA draft, it is important to share and discuss it with colleagues familiar with your context and students who will be asked to use the SCOBAs. Asking colleagues to review and students to use SCOBAs before introducing them to the classroom will give you feedback on both the conceptual representation and their usability. For example, Kurtz consulted a law professor and advanced LLM and SJD students with expertise in different law systems during SCOBA development and integrated their perspectives into subsequent drafts of the legal system SCOBAs. SCOBAs can always be revised and updated after use in the classroom, as well. Both Kurtz and Casal have revised the SCOBAs originally used in their dissertation studies to align with their current understanding of the concepts and to make them more usable for students.

Why and how do I gather students' prior knowledge of a concept

Research in second language writing has shown that understanding what students already know helps instructors adjust instruction appropriately and build meaningful connections between existing and new knowledge. This phase is critical in our Concept-Based Genre Writing pedagogy because it provides teachers insight into students' existing knowledge and awareness of language features, while helping students recognize how they currently understand and use these features in communication (Poehner & Lantolf, 2024). For teachers of multilingual writers, establishing students' pre-understanding reveals whether they are orienting to a genre relying on spontaneous concepts, or perhaps using scientific concepts from their home culture. Without a proper understanding of students' prior knowledge, an instructor risks overlooking nuanced differences between scientific presentations and students' existing conceptual understanding. For instance, when teaching sentence-level linguistic knowledge to mechanical engineering students, Qiu needed to elicit students' understanding of basic grammatical concepts (e.g. clause structure) before introducing more complex ones. Similarly, in Kurtz's context, where students were experts in one legal system but novices in another, understanding their knowledge of their home legal system was essential for effective instruction.

Schema-building activities, such as concept mapping (Ojima, 2006), have proven particularly effective in gathering this prior knowledge. They help make students' tacit knowledge explicit while preparing them for new learning. Through systematic observation of how students represent their understanding over time, instructors can track the evolution from spontaneous to scientific concepts. For example, you might ask students to create visual representations of their understanding of US common law, shell nouns, or grammatical stance in a reflective activity at different points in the instruction, documenting how their conceptualization becomes more systematic and aligned with disciplinary conventions. By engaging students in regular reflection on and revision of their conceptual models, you can support the internalization of scientific concepts while maintaining awareness of areas of dissonance where additional responsive mediation may be needed.

What makes an activity concrete and practical?

In V-SCT and C-BLI, 'concrete practical activity' (Lantolf & Poehner, 2014: 80) refers to goal-directed endeavors that have learners using and internalizing conceptual knowledge through mediated interaction. Activity can be seen as concrete and practical if it involves the use of target conceptual tools in the realization of an action that is goal-directed and purposeful, meaning that there is an identifiable communicative, physical, and/or cognitive outcome. In this sense, the activity is practical in that it requires the mobilization of explicit conceptual knowledge in functional practice. Ideally, activities are structured with the Zone of Proximal Development construct in mind, that is, projected beyond what learners can accomplish alone and designed in a manner that enables material and social mediation, such that a learner can accomplish the task with assistance. In this sense, through concrete practical activity, a learner may grow towards internalization of target concepts.

In a Concept-Based Genre Writing pedagogy, such activity is framed around writing. That can include analysis of writing to identify, scrutinize, and reflect on the affordances of target concepts as instantiated in text, revise or provide feedback on authentic writing for oneself or others, discuss writing goals, justify or explain choices in a piece of their own writing, or produce writing. Importantly, these tasks, if framed around scientific concepts and social genre practices, not only promote internalization of conceptual knowledge but also raise genre awareness and potentially cultivate a learner's relationship with a genre practice and the community in which it takes place.

How do I develop skills to work with students while they are languaging?

Responsivity or attunement in the Zone of Proximal Development is an important aspect of the collaborative activity, but can seem like an opaque skill. Mediation offered in Zone of Proximal Development activity is often described as a series of models, cues, questions, and hints provided to bridge the gap between what the learner can do today with support and what they might perform tomorrow independently. We can offer no template, no rigid structure for cues and support as Zone of Proximal Development activity is responsive, emergent, and dynamic. Questions, modeling, cues, hints, silence, and humor each have a place as a mediating strategy, dependent on the learner(s) at a particular time. For example, in Kurtz's chapters, the focal student Jun responded to silence. That is, early in the semester, Kurtz attuned to cues that Jun was thinking actively about her questions, so she allowed him the thinking time and space. By the end of the semester, a key feature in the quality of the interactions is that Kurtz's turns are much shorter and Jun is spending much less time thinking before responding.

In this volume, we originally intended to call ourselves Teacher-Researchers because that was how we conceptualize our role in our individual projects. (We are grateful it was pointed out to us how cumbersome this term was to read 198 times in the volume). One reason we initially adopted the term was that our development as mediators comes from both sides of the hyphen. Both experience teaching and engaging with research inform how we attune to the pasts of learners in the present moment and imagine with them a future where they agentively use the concepts we teach as psychological tools in writing. Just as with our students, developing skills as a mediator takes place over time, and is non-linear. To the extent possible, it is important to critically examine your classroom practices and the extent the provided mediation was attuned to students' current abilities and understandings. For example, part of Qiu's needs analysis was informed by his Mechanical Engineering colleague's investigation of student writing development. Or, during data collection, Kurtz shared excerpts of her mediation in IRAC 1 mediation sessions at a conference for works-in-progress. The feedback she received on her mediation proved invaluable in thinking through possible ways to develop as a mediator. Just as an important component of C-BLI is creating opportunities for development for our students, we must also consider how to create those opportunities for ourselves.

How does text analysis stimulate student verbalization/languaging?

In V-SCT, verbalization/languaging serves as a critical mediational tool that facilitates and traces learning development. As Gal'perin (1969) theorized, once an action is sufficiently learned through material support, it must be 'torn away' from this support and elevated to the verbal level, enabling learners to articulate their understanding explicitly (Lantolf & Thorne, 2006). Thus, verbalization/languaging activities require thought and preparation beyond asking learners to 'discuss.' Learners can (and should) be asked to explain concepts, what their definitions are, sure, but also how and why they have been used in a student's writing. These activities can occur verbally or in writing. Importantly in these tasks, the student's current understanding should be made visible to that student and, ideally, another. This externalization helps instructor and student alike understand current understanding so that attuned mediation can be provided to move the student towards fuller understanding and autonomous use of the concept in practical activity.

In a Concept-Based Genre Writing pedagogy, such activity often means text analysis. A text analysis engages learners in using course artifacts and conceptual understandings to identify, interpret, and reflect on target features in context. The (hypothetical) retroactive reconstruction and reflection through a text-based verbalization/languaging provide insights into learners' orientation to goal-directed activity and conceptual development. Our three dissertations demonstrate the versatility of text analysis in verbalization/languaging activities, though implemented under different names. Kurtz adopted dynamic assessment to gain access to and change students' understanding of writing US legal analysis after each IRAC essay they produced. Casal conducted text protocol meetings following instruction, while Qiu employed stimulated recall of screen recordings to examine student revision processes. Notably, Casal and Qiu enhanced their approach by comparing participants' linguistic choices against corpus data compiled for materialization activities.

To implement text-based verbalization effectively, instructors could approach it as a three-stage process where students become linguistic detectives of their own choices. The first stage begins with instructor preparation, comparing specific linguistic or rhetorical features with reference sources such as student essays in the corpus MICUSP or published research articles in Beijing Foreign Studies University CQPWeb. During the meeting, instructors should first invite participants to explain their topic and rhetorical choices (i.e. *'why did you write X in Y?'*), acting as responsive mediators who encourage explicit verbalization of decision-making rationales. The second stage involves collaborative text reading, where participants initiate a discussion of specific linguistic features that signal their rhetorical and functional aims. This can be enhanced through innovative approaches, such as Qiu's use of recorded revision process playback. After a round of reading, instructors could then take initiative to prompt the participants at the final stage to reflect on particular rhetorical, formal linguistic features, and revisions that were deemed salient in the preparation but had not been discussed by the participants.

How do I know if it's working? What does development look like?

As our studies have highlighted, assessing development in a Concept-Based Genre Writing pedagogy is not a simple matter of comparing student writing to target genre exemplars. In an important way, assessing development is a fundamental, dynamic, and on-going component of the pedagogy itself, as educators attune to learners moment-to-moment potentiality. This is complicated, but it is also the subject of considerable work on Dynamic Assessment and Responsive Mediation. However, we also offer some broader tips on what development may look like and how it can be gauged.

Development can be seen in evidence that learners are developing explicit understanding of the target concepts. This may include an understanding that relies on material or social mediation, with decreased reliance on mediation over time serving as a further sign of concept learning. Development can be seen in such change: moving away from pre-understandings, moving towards self-regulation, demonstrating new capacities or understandings. Crucial to detecting such changes is the verbalization/languaging phase of C-BLI, which serves as a site for growth and lens into learners' orientation to genre tasks and target concepts.

Our recommendation is that instructors in a Concept-Based Genre Writing pedagogy look more for changes in learners than they do for changes in texts themselves. While performance is an essential sign of development, it is important to evaluate such performance through the lens of learners' intentions. Learners may stumble into 'target-like' forms unintentionally, take-up formulas and resources to re-use uncritically, or otherwise create seemingly strong performance from time to time without having gained new psychological tools. Such occurrences do not suggest a transformation. At the same time, learners who acquire new ways of thinking about a genre task may still make 'non-target like' decisions that are expressions of agency and best understood through intentionality. And as a final point, development is non-linear, and learner writing is best analyzed within a broader context of performance and with insights into individualized motivations, intentions, and rationales.

Final Thoughts

Through this volume we have endeavored to motivate the integration of Concept-Based Language Instruction and genre-based writing pedagogy, lay out the premises of their integration, present three large-scale and innovative implementations of this pedagogy, and lay the groundwork for future implementations. The student participants in our studies demonstrated, generally speaking, considerable growth and development through these interventions. Perhaps more so than any of these students, we have benefited from the close analysis of and attention to target concepts and genre practices, educational relationships with our students, and the intellectual fellowship of negotiating and creating this volume. As in the pedagogy itself, we conclude our book by projecting towards the future and calling for others to innovate with this pedagogical framework in their contexts.

References

Abbuhl, R.J. (2005) The effect of feedback and instruction on writing quality: Legal writing and advanced L2 writers. Unpublished doctoral dissertation, Georgetown University.
Agar, M. (2002) *Language Shock: Understanding the Culture of Conversation* (Reprinted). Perennial.
Aktas, R.N. and Cortes, V. (2008) Shell nouns as cohesive devices in published and ESL student writing. *Journal of English for Academic Purposes* 7, 3–14.
Aljaafreh, A. and Lantolf, J.P. (1994) Negative feedback as regulation and second language learning in the zone of proximal development. *The Modern Language Journal* 78 (4), 465–483.
Anthony, L. (2019) AntConc (Version 3.5.8) [Computer Software]. Waseda University. Available from https://www.laurenceanthony.net/software
Araújo, J.C., Dieb, M. and Lima, S.D.C. (eds) (2010) Línguas na web: Links entre ensino e aprendizagem. *Ijuí, RS: Editora Unijuí*.
Artemeva, N. and Freedman, A. (2016) Everything is illuminated, or genre beyond the three traditions In N. Artemeva (ed.) *Genre Studies around the Globe: Beyond the Three Traditions* (pp. 1–9). Trafford Publishing.
Basturkmen, H. (2009) Commenting on results in published research articles and masters dissertations in language teaching. *Journal of English for Academic Purposes* 8, 241–251.
Basturkmen, H. (2011) A genre-based investigation of discussion sections of research articles in dentistry and disciplinary variation. *Journal of English for Academic Purposes* 11, 134–144.
Bawarshi, A.S. and Reiff, M.J. (2010) *Genre: An Introduction to the History, Theory, Research, and Pedagogy*. Parlor Press.
Bazerman, C. (1988) *Shaping Written Knowledge: The Genre and Activity of the Experimental Article in Science*. University of Wisconsin Press.
Bazerman, C. (1997) The life of genre, the life in the classroom. In W. Bishop and H. Ostrum (eds) *Genre and Writing* (pp. 19–26). Boynton/Cook.
Belcher, D. (2006) English for Specific Purposes: Teaching to the perceived needs and imagined futures in worlds of work, study, and everyday life. *TESOL Quarterly* 40 (1), 133–156.
Berkenkotter, C. and Huckin, T.N. (1995) *Genre Knowledge in Disciplinary Communication – Cognition/Culture/Power*. Lawrence Erlbaum Association.
Bhatia, V.K. (1993) *Analysing Genre: Language Use in Professional Settings*. Longman.
Bhatia, V.K. (2004) *Worlds of Written Discourse: A Genre-Based View*. Continuum.
Biber, D., Johansson, S., Leech, G., Conrad, S. and Finegan, E. (1999) *Longman Grammar of Spoken and Written English*. Longman.

Brown, A.L. and Campione, J.C. (1996) Psychological theory and the design of innovative learning environments: On procedures, principles, and systems. In R. Glaser (ed.) *Innovations in Learning: New Environments for Education* (pp. 289–325). Erlbaum.

Bruce, I. (2009) Results sections in sociology and organic chemistry articles: A genre analysis. *English for Specific Purposes* 28, 105–124.

Bruner, J., Goodnow, J. and Austin, G. (1956) *A Study of Thinking*. Chapman & Hall.

Buescher, K.D. (2015) Developing second language narrative literacy using concept-based instruction and a division-of-labor pedagogy. Unpublished doctoral dissertation, Pennsylvania State University.

Caldwell, C. (2009) *Lexical Vagueness in Student Writing: Are Shell Nouns the Problem?* Verlag Dr. Müller.

Caplan, N. and Farling, M. (2016) A dozen heads are better than one: Collaborative writing in genre-based pedagogy. *TESOL Journal* 8 (3), 564–581.

Casal, J.E. (2020) An integrated corpus and genre analysis approach to writing research and pedagogy: Development of graduate student genre knowledge. Unpublished doctoral dissertation, Pennsylvania State University.

Casal, J.E. and Kessler, M. (2020) Form and rhetorical function of phrase-frames in promotional writing: A corpus-and genre-based analysis. *System* 95, 102370.

Casal, J.E., Zhang, G., Matouq, I.I. and Alqabba, I.I. (2024) 'These results are inconsistent': 'This/these + shell noun' patterns in Engineering theses and research articles. *Journal of Second Language Studies* 7 (2), 320–346.

Charles, M. (2007) Argument or evidence? Disciplinary variation in the use of the Noun that pattern in stance construction. *English for Specific Purposes* 26 (2), 203–218

Charles, M. (2011) Using hands-on concordancing to teach rhetorical functions: Evaluation and implications for EAP writing classes. In A. Frankenberg-Garcia, L. Flowerdew and G. Aston (eds) *New Trends in Corpora and Language Learning* (pp. 26–43). Continuum.

Charles, M. (2024) Benefits and challenges of using do-it-yourself corpora for academic writing development. *TESOL Quarterly* 58 (3), 1205–1214.

Cheng, A. (2005) Genre and learning: Exploring learners and learning in the ESP genre-based framework of learning academic writing. Unpublished doctoral dissertation, Pennsylvania State University.

Chow, D.C.K. (2023) *The Legal System of the People's Republic of China in a Nutshell* (4th edn). West Academic Publishing.

Coffin, C. and Donahue, J.P. (2012) Academic literacies and systemic functional linguistics: How do they relate? *Journal of English for Academic Purposes* 11, 64–75.

Connery, M., John-Steiner, V. and Marjanovic-Shane, A. (2010) *Vygotsky and Creativity: A Cultural-Historical Approach to Play, Meaning, and the Arts*. Peter Lang.

Conrad, S. (2017) A comparison of practitioner and student writing in civil engineering. *Journal of Engineering Education* 106 (2), 191–217.

Cope, B. and Kalantzis, M. (eds) (1993) *The Powers of Literacy: A Genre Approach to Teaching Writing*. Falmer Press.

Cortes, V. (2013) The purpose of this study is to: Connecting lexical bundles and moves in research article introductions. *Journal of English for Academic Purposes* 12, 33–43.

Cumming, A. (1989) Writing expertise and second language proficiency. *Language Learning* 39 (1), 81–141.

Daly, M.C. (1998) What every lawyer needs to know about the civil law system. *The Professional Lawyer Symposium Issues*, 37–52.

Devitt, A.J. (1993) Generalizing about genre: New conceptions of an old concept. *College Composition & Communication* 44 (4), 573–586.

Devitt, A.J. (2004) *Writing Genres*. Southern Illinois University Press.

Díez Prados, M. (2018) Abstract nouns as metadiscursive shells in academic discourse. *Caplletra* 64, 153–178.

Durrant, P. and Mathews-Aydınlı, J. (2011) A function-first approach to identifying formulaic language in academic writing. *English for Specific Purposes* 30, 58–72.
Egan, K. (1998) *The Educated Mind: How Cognitive Tools Shape Our Understanding*. University of Chicago Press.
Esteve, O., Farró, L., Rodrigo, C. and Verdía, E. (2021) Meaningfully designing and implementing SCOBAs in socioculturally-based L2 teacher education programs. *Language and Sociocultural Theory* 8 (1), 8–34.
Feez, S. (2002) *Text-Based Syllabus Design*. Macquarie University.
Feez, S. and Joyce, D.S.H. (1998) *Text-Based Syllabus Design*. NCELTR and NSW AMES.
Feuerstein, R., Rand, Y. and Hoffman, M.B. (1979) *The Dynamic Assessment of Retarder Performers: The Learning Potential Assessment Device, Theory, Instruments, and Techniques*. University Park Press.
Fischl, R.M. and Paul, J.R. (1999) *Getting to Maybe: How to Excel on Law School Exams*. Carolina Academic Press.
Flowerdew, J. (1993) An educational, or process approach to the teaching of professional genres. *ELT Journal* 47 (4), 305–316.
Flowerdew, J. (2006) Use of signaling nouns in a learner corpus. *International Journal of Corpus Linguistics* 11 (3), 345–362.
Flowerdew, J. (2015) John Swales's approach to pedagogy in genre analysis: A perspective from 25 years on. *Journal of English for Academic Purposes* 19, 102–112.
Flowerdew, J. (2016) English for Specific Academic Purposes (ESAP) writing: Making the case. *Writing & Pedagogy* 8 (1), 5–32.
Flowerdew, L. (2020) The Academic Literacies approach to scholarly writing: A view through the lens of the ESP/Genre approach. *Studies in Higher Education* 45 (3), 579–591.
Flowerdew, J. and Forest, R.W. (2015) *Signaling Nouns in English: A Corpus-Based Discourse Approach*. Cambridge University Press.
Fogal, G.G. (2015) Pedagogical stylistics and concept-based instruction: An investigation into the development of voice in the academic writing of Japanese university students of English. Unpublished doctoral dissertation, University of Toronto.
Francis, G. (1986) *Anaphoric Nouns (Discourse Analysis Monograph)*. University of Birmingham.
Frawley, W. (1997) *Vygotsky and Cognitive Science. Language and the Unification of the Social and Computational Mind*. Harvard University Press.
Freedman, A. (1993) Show and tell? The role of explicit teaching in the learning of new genres. *Research in the Teaching of English* 27, 222–251.
Freedman, A. (1994) "Do as I say": The relationship between teaching and learning new genres. In A. Freedman and P. Medway (eds) *Genre and the New Rhetoric* (pp. 191–210). Taylor & Francis.
Freedman, A. (1999) Beyond the text: Towards understanding the teaching and learning of genres. *TESOL Quarterly* 33 (4), 764–767.
Freedman, A. and Medwey, P. (eds) (1994) *Genre and the New Rhetoric*. Taylor & Francis.
Gal'perin, P.Y.(1969) Stages in the development of mental acts. In M. Cole and I. Maltzman (eds), *A Handbook of Contemporary Soviet Psychology*(chapter 2). Basic Books.
Garner, B.A. and Black, H.C. (eds) (2019) *Black's Law Dictionary* (11th edn). Thomson Reuters.
Gencer, S. (2023) Development and use of flowchart for preservice chemistry teachers' problem solving on the first law of thermodynamics. *Journal of Chemical Education* 100 (9), 3393–3401.
Gieskes, K.E., McGrann, R.T. and DeRusso, C.G. (2012) Visual representations in mechanical engineering education. 2012 ASEE Annual Conference and Exposition, June, San Antonio, TX.

Gray, B. (2010) On the use of demonstrative pronouns and determiners as cohesive devices: A focus on sentence-initial this/these in academic prose. *Journal of English for Academic Purposes* 9 (3), 167–183.

Gray, B. and Cortes, V. (2011) Perception vs. evidence: An analysis of this and these in academic prose. *English for Specific Purposes* 30, 31–43.

Gray, B., Cotos, E. and Smith, J. (2020) Combining rhetorical move analysis with multidimensional analysis: Research writing across disciplines. In U. Römer, V. Cortes and E. Friginal (eds) *Advances in Corpus-Based Research on Academic Writing. Effects of Discipline, Register, and Writer Expertise* (pp. 138–168). John Benjamins.

Haenen, J., Schrijnemakers, H. and Stufkens, J. (2003) Sociocultural theory and the practice of teaching historical concepts. In A. Kozulin, B. Gindis, V.S. Ageyev and S.M. Miller (eds) *Vygotsky's Educational Theory in Cultural Context* (pp. 246–266). Cambridge University Press.

Halliday, M.A.K. and Hasan, R. (1976) *Cohesion in English*. Longman.

Hammond, J. and Macken-Horarik, M. (1999) Critical literacy: Challenges and questions for ESL classrooms. *TESOL Quarterly* 33 (3), 528–544.

Hammond, J., Burns, A., Joyce, H., Brosnan, D. and Gerot, L. (1992) *English for Social Purposes*. NCELTR.

Hartig, A.J. (2017) *Connecting Language and Disciplinary Knowledge in English for Specific Purposes: Case Studies in Law*. Multilingual Matters.

Hasselgård, H. (2012) Facts, ideas, questions, problems, and issues in advanced learners' English. *Nordic Journal of English Studies* 11 (1), 22–54.

Haverstick, A.D. (2024) *Dear 1L: Notes to Nurture a New Legal Writer*. Writing Law Tutors LLC.

Heiser, J. and Schikora, P.J. (2001) Process flowcharting: A key step to efficiency. *Journal of Professional Issues in Engineering Education and Practice* 127 (1), 24–29.

Hirano, E. (2009) Research article introductions in English for specific purposes: A comparison between Brazilian Portuguese and English. *English for Specific Purposes* 28, 240–250.

Hoffman, C. (2011) Using discourse analysis methodology to teach "Legal English". *International Journal of Law, Language, and Discourse* 1 (2), 1–19.

Hudson, T. (2007) *Teaching Second Language Reading*. Oxford University Press.

Hyland, K. (2000) *Disciplinary Discourses: Social Interactions in Academic Writing*. Pearson.

Hyland, K. (2005) *Metadiscourse: Exploring Interaction in Writing* (1st edn). Continuum.

Hyland, K. (2007) Genre pedagogy: Language, literacy and L2 writing instruction. *Journal of Second Language Writing* 16 (3), 148–164.

Hyon, S. (1996) Genre in three traditions: Implications for ESL. *TESOL Quarterly* 30, 693–722.

Hyon, S. (2017) *Introducing Genre and English for Specific Purposes*. Routledge.

Ivanič, R. (1991) Nouns in search of a context: A study of nouns with both open — And closed-system characteristics. *International Review of Applied Linguistics in Language Teaching* 29, 93–114.

Jian, H. (2010) The schematic structure of literature review in research articles of applied linguistics. *Chinese Journal of Applied Linguistics* 33 (5), 15–27.

Jiang, K.F. and Hyland, K. (2015) 'The fact that': Stance nouns in disciplinary writing. *Discourse Studies* 17, 529–550.

Jiang, K.F. and Hyland, K. (2018) Nouns and academic interactions: A neglected feature of metadiscourse. *Applied Linguistics* 39 (4), 508–531.

Jiang, K.F. and Hyland, K. (2021) 'The goal of this analysis.': Changing patterns of metadiscursive nouns in disciplinary writing. *Lingua* 252, 103017.

Jin, Y., Ni, Q., Wang, Y. and Zhou, M. (2022) Alignment of China's standards of English with the Common European Framework of Reference for Languages: A multilevel comparative analysis. *Language Assessment Quarterly* 19 (2), 157–177.

Johns, A.M. (1997) *Text, Role, and Context: Developing Academic Literacies*. Cambridge University Press.
Johns, A.M. (2011) The future of genre in L2 writing: Fundamental, but contested, instructional decisions. *Journal of Second Language Writing* 20 (1), 56–68.
Johnson, K. (2008) *Second Language Teacher Education: A Sociocultural Perspective*. Routledge.
Johnson, K. (2009) *Trends in Second Language Teacher Education*. Cambridge University Press.
Johnson, K. and Golombek, P. (2016) *Mindful L2 Teacher Education: A Sociocultural Perspective on Cultivating Teachers' Professional Development*. Routledge.
Joyce, B., Calhoun, M. and Hopkins, D. (1997) *Models of Learning – Tools for Teaching*. Open University Press.
Karpov, Y.V. (2003) Vygotsky's doctrine of scientific concepts: Its role for contemporary education. In A. Kozulin, B. Gindis, V.S. Ageyev and S.M. Miller (eds) *Vygotsky's Educational Theory in Cultural Context* (pp. 65–82). Cambridge University Press.
Karpov, Y.V. (2018) *Vygotsky's Theory of Cognitive Development*. Wiley.
Karpov, Y.V. and Gindis, B. (2000) Dynamic assessment of the level of internalization of elementary school children's problem-solving activity. In C. Lidz and J.G. Elliott (eds) *Dynamic Assessment: Prevailing Models and Applications* (pp. 133–154). JAI.
Kessler, M. and Casal, J.E. (2024) English writing instructors' use of theories, genres, and activities: A survey of teachers' beliefs and practices. *Journal of English for Academic Purposes* 69, 101384.
Kessler, M. and Polio, C. (2024) Introduction. In M. Kessler and C. Polio (eds) *Conducting Genre-Based Research in Applied Linguistics: A Methodological Guide* (pp. 1–10). Routledge.
Kim, J. (2013) Developing conceptual understanding of sarcasm in a second language through concept-based instruction. Unpublished doctoral dissertation, Pennsylvania State University.
Kozulin, A. (1998) *Psychological Tools: A Sociocultural Approach to Education*. Harvard University Press.
Kozulin, A. (2005) The concept of activity in Soviet psychology: Vygotsky, his disciples and critics. In H. Daniels (ed.) *An Introduction to Vygotsky* (pp. 102–123). Routledge.
Kurtz, L.M. (2017) "I don't know why. I just make comparisons.": Concept-based instruction to promote development of a second legal languaculture in international LL.M. students. Unpublished doctoral dissertation, Pennsylvania State University.
Kwan, B.S.C., Chan, H. and Lam, C. (2012) Evaluating prior scholarship in literature reviews of research articles: A comparative study of practices in two research paradigms. *English for Specific Purposes* 31, 188–201.
Lantolf, J.P. (ed.) (2000) *Sociocultural theory and second language learning*. Oxford University Press.
Lantolf, J.P. (2011a) The sociocultural approach to second language acquisition: Sociocultural theory, second language acquisition, and L2 development. In D. Atkinson (ed.) *Alternative Approaches to Second Language Acquisition* (pp. 24–47). Routledge.
Lantolf, J.P. (2011b) Integrating sociocultural theory and cognitive linguistics in the second language classroom. In E. Hinkel (ed.) *Handbook of Research in Second Language Teaching and Learning* (Vol. 2, pp. 303–318). Routledge.
Lantolf, J.P. and Yáñez, M.D.C. (2003) Talking yourself into Spanish: Intrapersonal communication and second language learning. *Hispania* 86, 97–109.
Lantolf, J.P. and Poehner, M.E. (2004) Dynamic assessment of L2 development: Bringing the past into the future. *Journal of Applied Linguistics* 1 (1), 49–72. https://doi.org/10.1558/japl.1.1.49.55872.
Lantolf, J.P. and Thorne, S.L. (2006) *Sociocultural Theory and the Genesis of Second Language Development*. Oxford University Press.

Lantolf, J.P. and Poehner, M.E. (2014) *Sociocultural Theory and the Pedagogical Imperative in L2 Education: Vygotskian Praxis and the Research/Practice Divide*. Routledge.

Lantolf, J.P., Kurtz, L.M. and Kisselev, O. (2017) Understanding the revolutionary character of L2 development in the ZPD: Why levels of mediation matter. *Language and Sociocultural Theory* 3, 177–196.

Laso, N.J. and John, S. (2013) A corpus-based analysis of the collocational patterning of adjectives with abstract nouns in medical English. In I. Verdaguer, N.J. Laso and D. Salazar (eds) *Biomedical English: A Corpus-Based Approach* (55–71). John Benjamins Publishing Company.

Le, T.N.P. and Harrington, M. (2015) Phraseology used to comment on results in the discussion section of applied linguistics quantitative research articles. *English for Specific Purposes* 39, 45–61.

Lee, D.S., Hall, C. and Barone, S.M. (2007) *American Legal English: Using Language in Legal Contexts* (2nd edn). University of Michigan Press.

Lindgren, E. and Sullivan, K.P.H. (2003) Stimulated recall as a trigger for increasing noticing and language awareness in the L2 writing classroom: A case study of two young female writers. *Language Awareness* 12 (3), 172–186.

Liu, Y. and Lu, X. (2020) N1 of N2 constructions in academic written discourse: A pattern grammar analysis. *Journal of English for Academic Purposes* 47, 1–11.

Lorés, R. (2004) On RA abstracts: From rhetorical structure to thematic organization. *English for Specific Purposes* 23, 280–302.

Lu, X., Yoon, J. and Kisselev, O. (2018) A phrase-frame list for social science research article introductions. *Journal of English for Academic Purposes* 36, 76–85.

Lu, X., Casal, J.E. and Liu, Y. (2020) The rhetorical functions of syntactically complex sentences in social science research article introductions. *Journal of English for Academic Purposes* 44, 1–16.

Marková, I. (1979) *The Social Context of Language*. John Wiley & Sons.

Martin, J.R. (1984) Language, register and genre. In F. Christie and J.R. Martin (eds) *Genre and Institutions: Social Processes in the Workplace and School* (pp. 3–39). Cassell.

Mercer, N. (2000) *Words and Minds: How We Use Language to Think Together*. Routledge.

Mertz, E. (2007) *The Language of Law School: Learning to Think Like a Lawyer*. Oxford University Press.

Miller, C.R. (1984) Genre as social action. *Quarterly Journal of Speech* 70, 151–167.

Miller, R. (2011) *Vygotsky in Perspective*. Cambridge University Press.

Molle, D. and Prior, P. (2008) Multimodal genre systems in EAP writing pedagogy: Reflecting on a needs analysis. *TESOL Quarterly* 42 (4), 541–566.

Murray, M.D. (2011) Explanatory synthesis and rule synthesis: A comparative civil law and common law analysis. *Bahcesehir Üniversitesi Hukuk Fakültesi-Kazanci Hukuk Dergisi* 83–84, 139–176.

Negretti, R. and McGrath, L. (2018) Scaffolding genre knowledge and metacognition: Insights from an L2 doctoral research writing course. *Journal of Second Language Writing* 40, 12–31.

Negueruela, E. (2003) A sociocultural approach to teaching and researching second languages: Systemic-theoretical instruction and second language development. Unpublished doctoral dissertation, Pennsylvania State University.

Negueruela, E. (2008) Revolutionary pedagogies: Learning that leads (to) second language development. In J. Lantolf and M. Poehner (eds) *Sociocultural Theory and the Teaching of Second Languages* (pp. 189–227). Equinox.

Nesi, H. and Gardner, S. (2012) *Genres Across the Disciplines: Student Writing in Higher Education*. Cambridge University Press.

Ojima, M. (2006) Concept mapping as pre-task planning: A case study of three Japanese ESL writers. *System* 34 (4), 566–585.

Omidian, T., Shahriari, H. and Siyanova-Chanturia, A. (2018) A cross-disciplinary investigation of multi-word expressions in the moves of research article abstracts. *Journal of English for Academic Purposes* 36, 1–14.

Paltridge, B. (2013) Genre and English for Specific Purposes. In B. Paltridge and S. Starfield (eds) *The Handbook of English for Specific Purposes* (pp. 389–409). Wiley-Blackwell.

Parkinson, J. (2011) The discussion section as argument: The language used to prove knowledge claims. *English for Specific Purposes* 30, 164–175.

Pho, P.D. (2008) Research article abstracts in applied linguistics and educational technology: A study of linguistic realizations of rhetorical structure and authorial stance. *Discourse Studies* 10 (2), 231–250.

Poehner, M.E. (2008a) Both sides of the conversation: The interplay between mediation and learner reciprocity in dynamic assessment. In J.P. Lantolf and M.E. Poehner (eds) *Sociocultural Theory and the Teaching of Second Languages* (pp. 33–56). Equinox.

Poehner, M.E. (2008b) *Dynamic Assessment. A Vygotskian Approach to Understanding and Promoting L2 Development*. Springer.

Poehner, M.E. and Lantolf, J.P. (2024) *Sociocultural Theory and Second Language Developmental Education*. Cambridge University Press.

Qiu, X. (2023) Writing in discipline-appropriate ways: An approach to teaching multilingual graduate students in mechanical engineering. Proceedings of 2023 ASEE Annual Conference & Exposition, June, Baltimore, MD.

Qiu, X. (2024a) Exploring the effect of corpus-based writing instruction on learner-corpus interaction in L2 revision: A study of Chinese EFL disciplinary writers. *TESOL Quarterly* 58 (3), 1108–1137.

Qiu, X. (2024b) A concept- and corpus-based instruction to promote effective communication in disciplinary research writing: Development of sentence-level linguistic knowledge in ESL/EFL graduate students. Unpublished doctoral dissertation, Pennsylvania State University.

Richards, K. (2003) *Qualitative Inquiry in TESOL*. Palgrave Macmillan.

Rothery, J. (1994) *Exploring Literacy in School English (Write it Right Resources for Literacy and Learning)*. Metropolitan East Disadvantaged Schools Program.

Saltzburg, S.A., Diamond, J.L., Kinports, K., Morawetz, T.H. and Little, R.K. (2009) *Criminal Law: Cases and Materials* (3rd edn). LexisNexis Matthew Bender.

Samraj, B. (2002) Introductions in research articles: Variations across disciplines. *English for Specific Purposes* 21, 1–17.

Samraj, B. (2005) An exploration of a genre set: Research article introductions in two disciplines. *English for Specific Purposes* 24 (2), 141–156.

Santos, M.B.D. (1996) The textual organization of research paper abstracts in applied linguistics. *Text-Interdisciplinary Journal for the Study of Discourse* 16 (4), 481–500.

Schanding, B. and Pae, H.K. (2018) Shell noun use in English argumentative essays by native speakers of Japanese, Turkish, and English. *International Journal of Learner Corpus Research* 4 (1), 54–81.

Schimel, J. (2012) *Writing Science: How to Write Papers That Get Cited and Proposals That Get Funded*. Oxford University Press.

Schmid, H-J. (2000) *English Abstract Nouns as Conceptual Shells: From Corpus to Cognition*. Mouton de Gruyter.

Serrano-Lopez, M. and Poehner, M. (2008) Materializing linguistic concepts through 3-D clay modeling: A tool-and-result approach to mediating L2 Spanish development. In J.P. Lantolf and M. Poehner (eds) *Sociocultural Theory and the Teaching of Second Languages* (pp. 321–346). Equinox.

Silver, C. (2005) Internationalizing U.S. legal education: A report on the education of transnational lawyers. *SSRN Electronic Journal*. https://doi.org/10.2139/ssrn.829744

Simpson-Vlach, R. and Ellis, N. C. (2010) An academic formulas list: New methods in phraseology research. *Applied Linguistics* 31 (4), 487–512.

Sing, C.S. (2013) Shell noun patterns in student writing in English for specific academic purposes. In S. Granger, G. Gilquin and F. Meunier (eds) *Twenty Years of Learner Corpus Research: Looking Back, Moving Ahead* (pp. 411–422). Presses Universitaires de Louvain.

Soler-Monreal, C., Corbonell-Olivares, M. and Gol-Salom, L. (2011) A contrastive study of the rhetorical organisation of English and Spanish PhD thesis introductions. *English for Specific Purposes* 30, 4–17.

Strong, S.I. and Desnoyer, B. (2016) *How to Write Law Exams: IRAC Perfected*. West Academic Publishing.

Swales, J.M. (1981) *Aspects of Article Introductions*. University of Michigan Press.

Swales, J.M. (1990) *Genre Analysis: English in Academic and Research Settings*. Cambridge University Press.

Swales, J.M. (2004) *Research Genres: Explorations and Applications*. Cambridge University Press.

Swales, J.M. (2011) Coda: Reflections on the future of genre and L2 writing. *Journal of Second Language Writing* 1 (20), 83–85.

Swales, J.M. (2012) A text and its commentaries: Toward a reception history of "genre in three traditions" (Hyon, 1996). *Ibérica* 24, 103–115.

Swales, J.M. and Lindemann, S. (2002) Teaching the literature review to international graduate students. In A. Johns (ed.) *Genre in the Classroom: Multiple Perspectives* (pp. 105–119). Lawrence Erlbaum.

Swaroop, T.R., Shivaprasad, C.M. and Rangappa, K.S. (2023) Art of writing flowchart in organic chemistry practicals induces logical thinking in chemistry students. *Journal of Chemical Education Research and Practice* 7 (1), 461–465.

Tan, Z. (2022) *Academic Writing for Engineering Publication*. Springer.

Tankó, G. (2017) Literary research article abstracts: An analysis of rhetorical moves and their linguistic realizations. *Journal of English for Academic Purposes* 27, 42–55.

Tardy, C.M. (2011) Genre analysis. In K. Hyland and B. Paltridge (eds) *Continuum Companion to Discourse Analysis* (pp. 54–68). Continuum.

Tardy, C.M. (2016) *Beyond Convention: Genre Innovation in Academic Writing*. University of Michigan Press.

Tardy, C.M. and Gevers, J. (2024) Genre, discourse, and second language research. In B. Paltridge and M.T. Prior (eds) *The Routledge Handbook of Second Language Acquisition and Discourse* (pp. 64–75). Routledge.

Tardy, C.M., Sommer-Farias, B. and Gevers, J. (2020) Teaching and researching genre knowledge: Toward an enhanced theoretical framework. *Written Communication* 37 (3), 287–321.

Thompson, G. and Ye, Y. (1991) Evaluation of reporting verbs used in academic papers. *Applied Linguistics* 12, 365–382.

Thornton, J.B. (2014) *U.S. Legal Reasoning, Writing, and Practice for International Lawyers*. LexisNexis.

Van Compernolle, R.A., Weber, A. and Gomez-Laichm M. (2016) Teaching L2 Spanish sociopragmatics through concepts: A classroom-based study. *The Modern Language Journal* 100 (1), 341–361.

Vian Jr., O. (2012) Beyond the three traditions in genre studies: A Brazilian perspective. Paper presented at Genre 2012 – Rethinking Genre 20 Years Later. An International Conference on Genre Studie, 26–29 June, Carleton University, Ottawa.

Vygotsky, L.S. (1978) *Mind in Society*. Harvard University Press.

Vygotsky, L.S. (1986) *Thought and Language* (A. Kozulin, ed. and trans.). MIT Press.

Vygotsky, L.S. (1987) *The Collected Works of L. S. Vygotsky: Vol. 1. Problems of General Psychology* (R.W. Rieber and A.S. Carton, eds, N. Minick, trans.). Plenum Press.

Walsh Marr, J. (2021) The promise and precarity of critical pedagogy in English for academic purposes. *BC Teal Journal* 6 (1), 132–141.

Wang, Y. and Hu, G. (2023) Shell noun phrases in scientific writing: A diachronic corpus-based study on research articles in chemical engineering. *English for Specific Purposes* 71, 178–190.

Wardle, E. (2009) "Mutt genres" and the goal of FYC: Can we help students write the genres of the university? *College Composition & Communication* 60 (4), 765–789.

Whalen-Bridge, H. (2008) Teaching common law reasoning to civil law students and the future of comparative legal skills. *Journal of Legal Education* 58, 364–371.

Wingate, U. and Tribble, C. (2012) The best of both worlds? Towards an English for academic purposes/academic literacies writing pedagogy. *Studies in Higher Education* 37 (4), 481–495.

Winter, S.L. (2001) *A Clearing in the Forest: Law, Life, and Mind*. University of Chicago Press.

Yang, R. and Allison, D. (2003) Research articles in applied linguistics: Moving from results to conclusions. *English for Specific Purposes* 22, 365–285.

Yoon, J. and Casal, J.E. (2020a) Rhetorical structure, sequence, and variation: A step-driven move analysis of applied linguistics conference abstracts. *International Journal of Applied Linguistics* 30 (3), 462–478.

Yoon, J. and Casal, J.E. (2020b) P-frames and rhetorical moves in applied linguistics conference abstracts. In U. Römer, V. Cortes and E. Friginal (eds) *Advances in Corpus-Based Research on Academic Writing: Effects of Discipline, Register, and Writer Expertise* (pp. 282–305). John Benjamins.

Index

Agency 2, 10, 12, 17, 20-21, 64, 66, 68, 69, 71, 74-75, 78
Analogical reasoning 25-26, 34-35, 36-37, 38-39, 41-54
AntConc 63, 70, 92, 105, 106, 110
Atlas.ti 99

Chinese 56, 82
Choice 2, 10, 12, 17, 20-21, 59, 63-64, 66, 68, 74, 76, 109, 115, 129, 131
Clausal subordination or subordination 83-84
Conceptual knowledge 63-64, 66, 68-69, 72-73, 75, 81
Concept presentation 16-17, 33-35, 57, 61, 70, 115
Concept selection 125
Concept-Based Genre Writing pedagogy 10, 20-21, 81, 117
Concept-Based Language Instruction 12, 16-20, 61-64, 68, 75, 82-83
Conceptual mediation 54, 120
Concrete practical activity 128
Corpus linguistics 55, 57, 61-63, 71
Corpus Query or CQ 91, 95

Development 36-37, 39-40, 63-67, 131
Dynamic assessment 35

English for Academic/Specific Purposes 7-11, 55-56, 59-60
Everyday concepts 15-17, 56
Explicit instruction 9-10, 16-17, 21, 61

Flowchart 88

Genre 2, 7-9, 20, 55, 57-60, 124
Genre analysis 60-63, 73
Genre awareness 8-12, 68-69, 74-76
Genre-based writing pedagogy 7-12
Grammatical Stance Expressions 84-85, 98, 102

Inter-Sentence Flow and Emphasis 84
Interviews/Text Protocols 65-67, 75-76, 79-80, 102
Intra-Sentence Discoursal Functions 84
IRAC essay 27-29

Kultura 99

Languaculture 23-25, 26-28
Legal analogy 38-39, 46, 47

Mechanical Engineering or ME 83
Mediation 12-15, 19, 35, 61, 64, 66, 68, 73, 79, 129
Metalanguage 70, 77, 79

Needs analysis 83-85

Perceptions of growth 122
Phases 121
    Orientation/pre-understanding 16-17, 32, 71-72, 76
    materialization 16-18, 33-35, 57, 61-63, 100, 115
    verbalization/languaging 16, 18-19, 35, 36, 61-64, 66, 71, 73, 79, 107, 110, 130
    performance 16, 19, 35-36, 100

143

internalization   14, 16-21, 36-37, 51, 53, 63, 66, 79
Internalized   23, 31, 32,
Practical, goal-oriented activity   35
Prior knowledge   101, 127
psychological tools   12-15, 20-21

Research Article or RA   56-57, 83
Responsive mediator   64, 66, 131
Revolutionary   13, 123
Rhetorical Genre Studies   7, 9-11
Rhetorical moves   9, 57, 59-61, 63, 72-76, 80-81

Scientific concepts   15-21, 56, 61, 125-126

SCOBA   17-19, 32-35, 62, 127
Screen recordings   96
Self-Assessment or SA   95
Self-regulation   14, 17-21, 66, 79, 81
Sentence Rewriting or SR   91, 95
Shell nouns   57-59, 62, 70-72, 77-78, 80
Social mediation   54, 120
Stimulated recall   96
Systemic Functional Linguistics   7-11

Teacher-researcher   1, 129
Text analysis   62-63, 130
Types of Clauses   84

Zone of Proximal Development   14, 54, 128, 129

For Product Safety Concerns and Information please contact our EU Authorised Representative:

Easy Access System Europe

Mustamäe tee 50

10621 Tallinn

Estonia

gpsr.requests@easproject.com

www.ingramcontent.com/pod-product-compliance
Lightning Source LLC
Chambersburg PA
CBHW052050300426
44117CB00012B/2063